Thomas Jefferson

Thomas Jefferson

MANUEL KOMROFF

MARSHALL CAVENDISH
CORPORATION

GREY CASTLE PRESS

Published by Grey Castle Press, Lakeville, Connecticut.

Marshall Cavendish Edition, North Bellmore, New York.

No part of this publication may be reproduced in whole or in part, or stored in a retrieval system, or transmitted in any form or by any means electronic, mechanical, photocopying, recording, or otherwise, without the written permission of Grey Castle Press.

Format, this edition, copyright © 1991 by Grey Castle Press.

Printed in the USA.

Library of Congress Cataloging-in-Publication Data

Komroff, Manuel, 1890–
    Thomas Jefferson / by Manuel Komroff.
      p.   cm. — (American cavalcade)
    Reprint. Originally published : New York : Messner, 1961.
    Includes bibliographical references and index.
    Summary: A biography of the Virginian who served as member of the Virginia House of Burgesses, member of the Second Continental Congress, writer of the Declaration of Independence, governor of Virginia, Secretary of State, and third president.
    ISBN 1-55905-083-7 (lg. print)
    1. Jefferson, Thomas, 1743–1826—Juvenile literature.   2. Presidents—United States—Biography—Juvenile literature.   3. Large type books. [1. Jefferson, Thomas, 1743–1826.   2. Presidents.   3. Large type books.]   I. Title.   II. Series.
[E332.79.K6 1991]
973.4'6'092—dc20
[B]
[92]   90-49177
                                                                                                 CIP
                                                                                                  AC

ISBN 1-55905-083-7
     1-55905-100-0 (set)

Photo Credits:

Cover: Library of Congress
Library of Congress—pgs. 36, 62, 81, 131
Brown Brothers—pg. 30
The Bettmann Archive—pg. 105
Thomas Jefferson Papers, Special Collections Department, Manuscript Division, University of Virginia Library—pg. 147 (top)
Printing Services Files, Special Collections Department, University Archives, University of Virginia Library—pg. 147 (bottom)
U.S. Department of the Interior, National Park Service, National Capital Region—pg. 153

Contents

★

Chapter 1	Childhood	7
Chapter 2	Williamsburg	18
Chapter 3	Lawyer and Burgess	28
Chapter 4	Romance	34
Chapter 5	Prelude to Independence	38
Chapter 6	Penman of Democracy	52
Chapter 7	Lawmaker	68
Chapter 8	Governor	72
Chapter 9	Monticello	80
Chapter 10	Ambassador to France	90
Chapter 11	Secretary of State	102
Chapter 12	An Interlude of Retreat	119
Chapter 13	Vice-President	124
Chapter 14	President	129
Chapter 15	The Sage of Monticello	143
For Further Reading		155
Index		157

Childhood

THE COLONY OF VIRGINIA, where Thomas Jefferson was born, stretched from the Atlantic coast far to the west and north. It was a vast territory, mostly wilderness, extending to the Mississippi and the Great Lakes and including the lands which today make up the states of Virginia, Kentucky, West Virginia, Ohio, Illinois, Indiana and parts of Michigan and Wisconsin.

Virginia was an English colony. It was founded by Sir Walter Raleigh under a grant from Queen Elizabeth and for its first 150 years, it retained strong ties both cultural and commercial with its mother country. It looked upon England as "home." Its young men were educated in England. The King of England appointed governors to rule Virginia, and the first legislature ever assembled on American soil was the Virginia House of Burgesses, which convened in the capital,

Williamsburg, and was patterned after England's Parliament.

The early settlers who came to Virginia from England made their homes along the coast. Then, as tobacco became more popular in Europe and the demand for this Indian weed increased, the settlers moved slowly inland, clearing the fertile land along the many rivers and inlets of the coast and creating plantations, some covering 50,000 acres or more.

By 1700, the coastal plain of Virginia, or Tidewater country as it came to be known, was a vast area of rich slaveholding plantations. The homes were large and surrounded by beautiful gardens. The ships from England, which picked up the great cargoes of tobacco, brought to the wealthy Virginia planters all the latest styles, books and papers as well as elegant carriages and coaches and luxurious furniture, silver, china, carpets and silk drapes, to furnish their great houses.

The planters and their families patterned themselves after the aristocrats of England. They were educated, traveled and loved music. They wore silks, ruffles and lace and powdered wigs. They were courteous, displayed polished manners and observed a European system of rank with all its expressions of respect. They kept horses, went hunting, gambled, drank heavily and bet on horse races and cockfights. They entertained lavishly.

But all the people of Virginia Colony were not rich tobacco planters. There were the thousands of Negro slaves and indentured servants who worked the plantations, and on the western fringe of the Tidewater country there were some farmers and a few tradesmen and artisans. These people were poor and, while they too patterned themselves after the English, they lived in simple houses and wore plain clothes made of homespun.

As time went on and the flat coastal lands were all taken, the new settlers who came to Virginia pushed farther inland toward the Appalachian Mountains and carved out their farms and plantations on the edge of a great wilderness known as the Up Country. Here life was much harder than in the Tidewater district. There were Indians and the land was hilly and heavily forested. The rivers were narrow and too shallow for the English ocean-going boats to navigate. Roads were few and very rugged, so the Up Country settlers were cut off from their fellow Virginians on the coast and their motherland, England. Their lives were similar to those of the frontiersmen of the other colonies. They lived in log cabins, wore buckskin shirts and coonskin caps and hunted for much of their food.

Such was the Colony of Virginia when Peter Jefferson, Thomas Jefferson's father, grew to manhood and started out in life for himself.

Peter Jefferson was born in 1707 into one of those middle-class families which lived in the area situated between the rich Tidewater and the wilderness of the Up Country. His forefathers were some of the first settlers of Virginia, having come from Wales even before the Mayflower touched our shores.

Peter Jefferson had received no schooling but had educated himself. He read all the finest books that he could get hold of, including works on science. He taught himself mathematics, became a surveyor, and was held in such high regard by his neighbors that when he was only twenty-four he was appointed as a magistrate of Goochland County, where he lived. He also served as sheriff. However, in spite of these duties, he continued his work as surveyor, traveling about the Tidewater lands and their fringe areas as he was needed. He loved the outdoors. He was a friend of the Indians. And he could survey in the wilderness, day after day, living on wild game and sleeping at night in the hollow of a tree.

When Peter Jefferson was thirty years old a wonderful opportunity presented itself. The Indians, under pressure from the white settlers, abandoned the Up Country and moved westward, freeing vast areas of fertile land; all a man now had to do was stake out a claim and the land was his. And Peter Jefferson together with his best friend, William Randolph, a young widower with three small children, were two of the very first to head into the Up Country.

Peter and William followed the James River westward. After several days they came to a great plantation owned by William Randolph's uncle. Here they remained for a while as guests and here Peter met William's cousin, Jane Randolph, who later became his wife.

Peter and William followed a small river, called the Rivanna, up into the wilderness until they came to suitable land. Then each staked out a claim, William on one side of the Rivanna and Peter on the other. But William Randolph did not want the river to separate them and since Peter could not find a proper place for a home on his claim, he insisted upon giving Peter a building site of 400 acres on his side of the Rivanna. To seal the bargain, Peter Jefferson was to pay William Randolph "the biggest bowl of arrack punch" the Raleigh Tavern in Williamsburg could supply.

Peter was eager to start clearing his land and building a house. He wanted to start raising tobacco as soon as possible. This meant that he had to make numerous trips back to the Tidewater country for materials and slaves.

Jane Randolph had grown up in great luxury and Peter could not possibly give her what she had always known. But they loved each other, and so after two years, when Peter had completed a simple but comfortable house, they were married. Peter was thirty-two, Jane nineteen.

Immediately following the marriage Peter and Jane started out for their wilderness home which he named "Shadwell."

A daughter, Jane, was the first child born at Shadwell. Then came Mary, and on April 13, 1743, a son, Thomas: Thomas Jefferson.

The land rush to the Up Country was so great that Jane and Peter soon had neighbors. Since there was the constant fear of attacks by the Indians and French who were in the Ohio Territory, Peter joined the militia, serving as a lieutenant colonel. He was under the command of a surveyor named Joshua Fry, a professor at William and Mary College in Williamsburg.

Peter was very busy, but nothing interfered with his friendship with William Randolph. The two saw each other almost every week. Then came a tragic day that ended the long and cherished association. William Randolph died. This brought about a great change in the Jefferson family because William's last wish was that Peter and his family move to Tuckahoe so that Peter and Jane could supervise the upbringing and education of his orphaned children.

So Peter and Jane Jefferson and their three small children and a new baby, Elizabeth, moved to Tuckahoe, a luxurious manor house and plantation in the Tidewater district.

Thomas Jefferson was just two years old, and he spent the next seven years in this cultured and fashionable world.

At Tuckahoe, Tom's activities were typical of all Tidewater boys. He learned to ride, hunt and swim; to play the violin and dance minuets and reels.

But life was not all play and parties for the young boy; it was at Tuckahoe that Tom's formal education began. At the age of five he started classes in a little private schoolhouse on the plantation, where the Randolph children and his sisters were already in attendance. From the very first Tom proved to be quick and apt in his studies.

After four years of training in reading, writing and arithmetic, when Tom was nine, his father reached two important decisions: one, since the Randolph children were now grown, he and his family could move back to Shadwell. And hoping to give his son the education which he had missed, he decided to send Tom away to a good school.

So in 1752 the Jeffersons went back to Albemarle county in the primitive Up Country, and Tom went off to live and study with the Rev. William Douglas, a Scotch clergyman who taught French, Latin and Greek.

Peter Jefferson had not neglected Shadwell during the seven years he and his family had lived in Tuckahoe. More land had been acquired, cleared and put under cultivation and two large wings had been added to the house.

Neither had he neglected his studies and work. During those same seven years Peter had continued to read all he could find and he had worked with Prof. Joshua Fry surveying the boundary between Virginia and North Carolina. Then when Prof. Fry died, leaving his command in the militia to a young colonel named George Washington, Peter Jefferson had been sent in Fry's place as representative from Albemarle county to the House of Burgesses in Williamsburg. Returning to Shadwell, he was now chosen as governor of Albemarle county.

So life was good for the Jeffersons. There were honors and prosperity. Young Tom, home for his vacations, grew to love Shadwell with a love that lasted all his life.

Here young Tom entered into a new and wonderful world, completely different from that which he had known at Tuckahoe. Shadwell with its great tobacco fields stood at the edge of the wilderness—a land to be explored and loved: a land of beautiful trees and plants, a land of birds, deer, bear, panther, wolves and wild turkeys. A land where Indians and buffaloes still wandered.

Peter Jefferson was eager that his young son should have a formal education, but there were other things he should know, things which could not be learned in a classroom. So he and Tom spent many hours and days together, and from his pioneer father, Tom learned about hard work, self-reliance and self-discipline. He also learned to love the wondrous world about him.

But these joyous days together came to a sudden end. Peter Jefferson died. This at once changed

Tom's life. As the eldest son and in accordance with English law followed in the Virginia colony, he inherited Shadwell with its thousands of acres, buildings, and slaves. Although he was only fourteen he became the head of the family, which consisted of his widowed mother, six sisters, and a baby brother named Randolph.

Peter Jefferson had provided well for his family. Shadwell was a prosperous plantation, and he had left a guardian to attend to its welfare and theirs. So life went on in much the same pleasant manner as before. And according to Peter Jefferson's wishes Tom's education continued.

Completing his studies with the Rev. Douglas, Tom was now sent to live and study with the Rev. James Maury, a classical scholar who ran a log-cabin school just fourteen miles from Shadwell.

Tom attended Rev. Maury's school for two years, and during his vacations he always returned to Shadwell. He spent his days supervising the plantation and roaming the forests. Instead of his father, his companion now was Dabney Carr, a boy from a neighboring plantation. They were of the same age and had many interests in common.

Often they would go to Tom's favorite spot, the top of a little mountain situated on the other side of the Rivanna from Shadwell, on the very land which Peter Jefferson had originally staked out as his claim. Here they would sit beneath a great oak, dreaming and planning their future. Here, on the top of this little mountain, Tom said he would someday build a great house. And here, beneath the big oak, he and Dabney would be buried side by side. To this they vowed a solemn vow.

Williamsburg

THOMAS JEFFERSON completed his classical studies at Dr. Maury's when he was sixteen, and after a few months' stay at Shadwell, left for the College of William and Mary in Williamsburg, a hundred and twenty miles away. "By going to college, I shall get a more universal acquaintance, which may thereafter be serviceable to me," he wrote in one of his letters. "And I suppose I can pursue my studies in the Greek and the Latin as well there as here, and likewise learn something of the mathematics."

At sixteen Jefferson was already six feet tall. He was broad shouldered and slender. His neck was long and thin. His face was freckled and with a reddish tint, his jaw square and firm and his nose well chiseled but with a sudden tilt at the very end. His hair was red, and his eyes were intelligent, soft and gray-blue. His voice was quiet and well modulated. His manner, pleasant and enthusiastic. All in all, he was not handsome, but he had great charm.

Williamsburg was far away, a long journey on horseback through forests and across streams where there were no bridges. But this did not trouble Tom, who loved the wild country. When he came to a plantation he would stop, as was the custom of the time, and spend a few days with the planter and his family, some of whom had known his father.

It was during just such an evening at the plantation home of a Colonel Dandridge, as Tom was going to Williamsburg that first time, that he met a strange young man who was to become his lifelong friend. He was nine years older than Tom. His speech was plain, his manners ordinary, his clothes coarse. He was rather boisterous but likable. He lacked the polish of a gentleman, but he possessed a vitality which attracted Jefferson. His name was Patrick Henry.

Williamsburg was a town of only two hundred houses and a thousand people, but it was the largest place Thomas Jefferson had ever seen.

The Duke of Gloucester Street, its one handsome street, formed the larger part of the town. It was almost a mile long and lined on both sides with beautiful trees. A fine brick Capitol building, which contained the House of Burgesses and the Courts of Law, stood proudly at one end while the College of William and Mary stood at the other end. And halfway between, set back from the street and surrounded by gardens, was the magnificent Palace in which the King's governor resided.

The rest of the Duke of Gloucester Street was taken up with homes, stores and the Raleigh Tavern, the very place where Peter Jefferson paid his friend William Randolph the great "bowl of arrack punch" for the land on which Shadwell now stood. Here, at the Raleigh Tavern, much of Williamsburg's gay life centered.

Tom had known this sort of life as a child when he lived in Tuckahoe, so he looked forward to staying in Williamsburg. But he also looked forward to the cultural side of Williamsburg. Since it was the capital of the Virginia colony, brilliant men of culture, men who possessed keen political judgment came from all parts of populated Virginia. He knew that these men rivaled the most learned men in the colonies.

The College of William and Mary had been founded by King James the First of England as a school for Indians, but by the spring of 1760 this original purpose had been altered, and William and Mary consisted of a grammar school, high school and college attended almost exclusively by white Virginians.

It was staffed by the president and two professors; one taught rhetoric, logic and ethics, and the other, a Dr. Small, taught mathematics and science.

To enter this college a young man was required to take an oral examination conducted by the two college professors, the president, and a minister who was a student of Greek and Latin. Young Tom, who had just celebrated his seventeenth birthday, proved so brilliant that he was immediately admitted into the third-year class. He skipped the first two years.

Promising as he was, Tom's college days might have been wasted because the other students were not serious. Tom, who was young and eager for fun, might easily have slipped into an idle life of sports and pleasure had it not been for Dr. Small, who took an immediate liking to him and became his intimate friend.

In later years Tom wrote that Dr. Small was "a man profound in most of the useful branches of science, with a happy talent of communication, correct and gentlemanly manners, and an enlarged and liberal mind. He, most happily for me, became soon attached to me, and made me his daily companion. . . . From his conversations I got my first views of the expansion of science, and the system of things in which we are placed."

Dr. Small had been born in Scotland and was a friend of the scientist, Erasmus Darwin, a name that his grandson Charles Darwin was to make famous. He was also a friend of James Watt, who, some years later, was to invent the steam engine.

Here in Williamsburg Dr. Small knew all the most interesting and important people. He was a close friend of Francis Fauquier, governor of the Virginia colony, who lived in the great brick palace halfway down the Duke of Gloucester Street. He was also the friend of George Wythe, one of the most distinguished lawyers in Virginia. And he introduced his young red-haired friend to both of these unusual men.

Fauquier, besides being a most charming person, was interested in physics and was a Fellow of the Royal Society, the English society of scientists. He had also written a very successful book on public finances. To Jefferson's delight he played the violin.

The lawyer, George Wythe, was a classical scholar and possessed great learning in astronomy, mathematics, and science. He was also a true liberal, believing firmly in a republican form of government.

The friendship between Jefferson and Wythe, which was born at this time, was to last many, many years, ending only with the death of Wythe. Jefferson was then President of the United States, and in his will Wythe left him his fine library, his goldheaded cane, his silver cups, and some other cherished possessions.

The four friends made an odd quartet: the Royal Governor of Virginia, the distinguished Dr. Small, the eminent lawyer George Wythe and the seventeen-year-old Thomas Jefferson. There must certainly have been something most remarkable about Jefferson even at that early age, that at seventeen he should be accepted as a close friend of three of Virginia's ablest men.

Later Jefferson was to pay these three men a great compliment. He said that he tried to model himself after them and that they "probably fixed the destinies of my life."

When he was only nineteen, after completing his studies at William and Mary, Jefferson decided to study law. George Wythe accepted him as a student and brought him into his Williamsburg law office.

There were no law schools in those days and

young men prepared for the bar by studying on their own and working under some accredited lawyer. They helped prepare the cases, attended court sessions, and read standard books on law. Then when they and their sponsors felt they were ready they appeared before a special board of examiners. If they passed they were then licensed and could enter into the practice of law under their own names.

Tom allowed himself five years for this preparation. Besides training in law under George Wythe he also planned to study history, political science, philosophy, Spanish, Italian, German and some American Indian languages. He felt that such a background would make him a much finer lawyer, and he stuck to his plan for five years, working ten to fifteen hours a day. He persisted with this monumental program for five years even though he knew many young men, including his friends Patrick Henry and Dabney Carr, had completed their law studies in much less time. Patrick Henry completed his in only six months.

During these same five years Jefferson also read books on botany, agriculture, chemistry, ethics, and religion. To supplement this reading, he kept notebooks in which he recorded things of interest, a practice he continued throughout his life. He made notes on such widely differing subjects as parliamentary law and the changes of the seasons in Virginia. Each day he noted down the temperature and the direction of the wind; when the first snow occurred in the fall and when the first strawberries ripened in spring. There wasn't a single subject he did not investigate. At this time Jefferson also read the English novelists and other important classical works, many of them in their original languages.

Despite his heavy program, he kept up with his other interests. He practiced his violin every day, he attended the House of Burgesses to listen to the proceedings, he superintended his plantation at Shadwell, and like the other young men of his time he attended horse races, parties, and dances.

On April 13, 1764 Jefferson celebrated his twenty-first birthday. He was in Williamsburg at the time studying law, and like all the other intelligent and educated people in the colonies, he was much concerned over the strained relations between the thirteen American colonies and the mother country, England.

The colonies were growing stronger and more prosperous every day. They needed more and more freedom and self-determination, but King George the Third and his Parliament did not recognize this. Many misunderstandings arose, but the most serious concerned taxation.

Some years before, the French and Indians in the Ohio Territory had come into open conflict with the colonists. War had followed but in the end England and her American colonies won the conflict, and France had been forced to surrender Canada and all her lands east of the Mississippi. France had retained only the city of New Orleans and Louisiana, a vast wilderness which stretched north and west of the Mississippi River.

England was victorious but exhausted by the financial drain, and she felt that the colonies should help pay the costs. Therefore she planned to collect money by demanding that a tax be paid on and a stamp be affixed to all papers and documents, used in the colonies.

When this news reached America, a murmur of protest was heard from New Hampshire through Georgia. But England did not heed the warning. The colonies were weak, and she was strong, so early in 1765 Parliament passed the Stamp Act. What had been a murmur now became indignation and anger.

However, all suddenly changed when the House of Burgesses met in Williamsburg that spring. Toward the end of the session its newest member, Patrick Henry, rose to speak on the one subject which was on every member's mind but which few had even dared to mention, "taxation without representation."

His words and eloquence electrified all present. He ended his fiery protest by crying out, "Caesar had his Brutus, Charles the First his Cromwell, and George the Third . . ." At the mention of the king the hall echoed with shouts of "Treason! Treason!" But Patrick Henry would not be silenced. He continued in a loud, clear voice, "And George the Third may profit by their examples. If this be treason, make the most of it."

In the excitement that followed, the House of Burgesses passed all six resolutions. Then Patrick Henry, the hero of the day, left the hall, mounted his horse and rode home.

Young Thomas Jefferson, was in the House of Burgesses that day. He was standing in the doorway and this eloquent burst of oratory made a deep impression upon him. Many years later he recalled Patrick Henry's talents as an orator: "They were great indeed; such as I have never heard from any other man. He appeared to me to speak as Homer wrote."

Lawyer and Burgess

THOMAS JEFFERSON was admitted to the bar in the spring of 1767. He entered practice at once, and although he now made Shadwell his home like the other lawyers of the time he traveled all over the Virginia colony, trying cases wherever his services were needed.

Jefferson proved to be unusually successful from the very start. During his first year he had sixty-four cases, and four years later he tried over four hundred cases. Very few lawyers in Virginia had larger practices.

Jefferson's law practice occupied much of his time, but not all. He still followed his many interests, and he added a new one to his life. As a boy he had dreamed of building a great house on the top of his mountain. He would now build the most beautiful home in all Virginia, and he would call it Monticello, "little mountain" in Italian.

His friends Fauquier, Wythe and Small had introduced him to the world of Greek, Roman, and European architecture. They had spoken of these wonders, had shown him etchings and drawings, and had lent him books on the subject. He had decided that he would create a great house of classical design surrounded by beautiful gardens and wooded parks. The outbuildings would be modeled after Greek temples, and there would be flowers, hidden grottoes, fountains, fern-decked springs. It would be the haven of every wild creature of the forest, including even a great buck elk.

During his college days, Jefferson had his men build a road up his mountain and level off the top. Since there were no architects in Virginia at that time, he had begun drawing up his own plans. Although he had never had lessons in art, he had a natural gift for drawing.

Monticello was ever in his thoughts, and whenever he had a spare moment he jotted down his ideas in a notebook that he always had at hand. Floor plans and elevations were drawn. There would be many rooms, over thirty. The family quarters would be on the first, second and third floors. The kitchen, laundry, icehouse,

Jefferson began his career in politics—and the fight for freedom—as a young member of the Virginia House of Burgesses. Other representatives in that body included Thomas Payne and George Washington.

storerooms, and servants' quarters would be concealed in the basement beneath the house and its gracious terraces. There would be underground passages leading to the stables and carriage house. Details and ornaments were designed.

The beds would all be built in; his own bed would be under an arch between his bedroom and library so that upon awakening he could enter whichever room he chose. And it would be so arranged that during the day the bed could be raised by ropes to the ceiling, leaving a passage between his library and bedroom. There would also be dumbwaiters from the library and dining room to the kitchen so that he could be served food and drink at any time and without delay. Nothing was overlooked. He even drew up plans for the gardens, groves, and walks.

He was completely absorbed in the planning and building of Monticello, when suddenly in 1768 England struck at the colonies. Disregarding the lessons learned from the Stamp Act, Parliament passed the Townshend Acts, which, among other things, put a tax upon glass, paper, and tea. This was another example of "taxation without representation," and the colonies once more murmured against this injustice.

Jefferson now entered the fray. He ran as representative from Albemarle County, won the election and went to Williamsburg to take his seat in the House of Burgesses, along with his friend Patrick Henry and the wealthy planter and hero of the French and Indian War, George Washington.

From its opening moments this session of the House of Burgesses was a tense and spirited one. Resolution after resolution was introduced and passed. One resolution asked that the colonies, all thirteen of them, join together and act as one in dealing with England about their grievances.

Governor Fauquier was dead, and the new governor immediately dissolved the defiant House of Burgesses. As representative of the king he had no other choice. But his action only fanned the embers of discontent.

The House of Burgesses had been dissolved, but its members were not to be suppressed. A large number of them, including George Washington, Patrick Henry and Thomas Jefferson, met the next day in the Apollo Room of the Raleigh Tavern and devised a plan for striking back at England. They drew up a proposal to boycott English goods until England, through her loss of trade with the American colonies, should repeal the Townshend Acts and agree never again to use such arbitrary measures.

Strangely enough the governor, in spite of his action, sided with the colonists. He wrote immediately to England asking for moderation. Parliament listened to his advice, promising that the wrongs would be righted, and that the Townshend Act would be rescinded; there would be no more "taxation without representation." Everyone was satisfied, and a new House of Burgesses convened.

But Parliament did not do as it had promised. Although the Townshend Act was repealed the tax on tea continued. However, few people, besides Thomas Jefferson, realized the danger which still existed.

Thomas Jefferson was twenty-six years old when he was first elected to the House of Burgesses. This marked a turning point in his life. By his election to the House of Burgesses he was plunged into the fight for freedom.

Through books he had been educated by the greatest minds of all time. He had learned from his reading of Greek, Roman, and European classics to see far beyond the narrow confines of everyday living and to envisage a state where the common man would be supreme. And so from the moment of his election he became an open champion of the rights of man. From that moment on, he devoted his long life to man, to freedom and to democracy. It was indeed a decisive moment; a moment that changed the history of the world.

Romance

ONE DAY IN THE EARLY SPRING of 1770, while Jefferson and his mother were visiting some Up Country neighbors, Shadwell burned to the ground. One of Jefferson's slaves came running with the bad news.

The loss of Shadwell naturally brought changes in the lives of Jefferson and his family. His mother, sisters, and brother were forced to move into the overseer's house, while Jefferson moved into a one-room building-shed on the top of his little mountain. In a letter to a friend he said, "I have here but one room, which like the cobbler's serves me for parlor, for kitchen and hall. I may add, for bedchamber and study, too."

But these crowded quarters did not bother him; his one real concern was his lost library. It had contained all the books he had inherited from his father, all his law books, as well as books which he had carefully selected and bought since his youth. But he was not one to sit idle and complain. He set to work at once to replace them. He sent lists of titles to England, and within two years he had 1,250 volumes.

Living in the building-shed was certainly not very comfortable, so it was imperative to speed up the work on Monticello. For the next year Jefferson gave it his undivided attention. It was an enormous job, for in those days one did not go to a lumber yard to buy supplies. Trees had to be cut in the forest and hewn into beams or sawed into boards; clay had to be shaped and baked into bricks, and nails had to be wrought. Jefferson supervised all this work. He established workshops and taught his slaves how to make bricks and nails and other essentials. He showed them how to set windows and doors and lay parquet floors. After a full year of hard work the main house was still on paper; only one wing, or pavilion, had been completed.

Back in Williamsburg Thomas Jefferson had a friend, John Wayles, a prominent lawyer. Wayles invited Jefferson to visit him at his plantation home just outside of Williamsburg. It was there that Jefferson met one of Wayles' daughters, a young widow, Martha Skelton.

Jefferson married Martha Wayles Skelton on Jan. 1, 1772. They had six children, but only two lived to maturity. Mrs. Jefferson died ten years after their marriage, and Thomas never remarried.

Martha was so intelligent and well educated she was a perfect companion for the brilliant young man. They could share so much, including their passionate love of music. So a year after their first meeting, on New Year's Day, 1772, they were married.

Jefferson spent most of the first year of his marriage at Monticello with his bride. Putting politics and law aside, he lived the life he loved, rising early each morning and dividing the day among his many interests. Each afternoon, between one and three, he rode out on one of his thoroughbred horses and in the evenings he turned to music, the "passion of my life" as he called it. He played the violin while Mrs. Jefferson played upon a harpsichord that he had imported from Europe as a gift for her.

This was a happy year, and before it ended Jefferson and his wife celebrated the birth of their first child, a little girl. They named her Martha after her mother.

5

Prelude to Independence

THOMAS AND MARTHA JEFFERSON were an extremely happy couple. And it is possible that when the first year of their marriage ended Jefferson thought that he would spend the rest of his life at Monticello surrounded by the things he loved, his wife and baby, his books and violin, his gardens and pure-blooded horses. But this was not to be. The troubles between the colonies and England increased, and Jefferson was drawn into the conflict.

For some time past a British man-of-war, the *Gaspee*, had been stationed off the coast of Rhode Island, for the purpose of wiping out lucrative smuggling that the colonists were doing. The commander of the *Gaspee* stopped all ships leaving Newport and Providence and without a warrant boarded and searched them.

Now the colonists felt that England's revenue

laws were unjust and that they were entitled to engage in smuggling, and they considered the commander's action as pure piracy. One night, when it was learned that the *Gaspee* had run aground, a group of men rowed with muffled oars to the helpless ship, captured the commander and crew and set the *Gaspee* on fire.

The king was shocked by this violence. Parliament quickly passed an act stating that, henceforth, anyone in the colonies accused of destroying even so small a thing as a "button on a mariner's coat" would be guilty of a crime punishable by death and would be taken to England for trial.

Parliament's act proved to be a great mistake, because what had been a purely local incident between the colony of Rhode Island and England, now became the direct concern of all the thirteen colonies including Virginia. When Jefferson took his seat in the House of Burgesses in the late winter of 1773, the air was charged with tension.

The members of the House of Burgesses could speak of nothing but the "*Gaspee* incident" and how Virginia could most effectively protest to the Crown.

However, their talk and debates seemed confused, leading nowhere, and so some of the younger and more liberal members, Thomas

Jefferson, Patrick Henry and two brothers, Richard and Francis Lee, decided to meet privately at the Raleigh Tavern to formulate a plan of action. Dabney Carr also joined them. He had recently married one of Jefferson's sisters and had just been elected to the House of Burgesses.

These young men felt that the colonies separated by long distances, north to south, could be strong only if united. They felt that it was imperative for the colonies to act together; the problems of one should be the concern of all thirteen. Jefferson has himself written: "We were all sensible that the most urgent of all measures was . . . to produce a unity of action."

With this aim they decided to urge their fellow members in the House of Burgesses to adopt an idea which was also being suggested by two patriots in Massachusetts, John and Samuel Adams. They recommended the formation of Committees of Correspondence in each of the colonies. The purpose of these committees would be to notify one another of all important happenings. Thus a paper bridge of information would join the colonies together. A "unity of action" would result.

Jefferson, who had a genius for practical purposes, drew up a series of resolutions presenting their plan. But since he was a poor speaker he asked Dabney Carr, whom he considered the best orator next to Patrick Henry, to present them the next morning in a speech to the House of Burgesses.

Jefferson's resolutions were promptly passed and he himself was made a member of the Virginia Committee of Correspondence. He was also appointed, together with Dabney Carr and Patrick Henry, to present the idea to the other colonies.

When the royal governor heard what had happened he immediately dissolved the House of Burgesses. However this did not stop Thomas Jefferson and his friends. They met the very next day at the Raleigh Tavern and letters explaining the purpose of the Committees of Correspondence were drawn up and immediately dispatched to the other colonies by fast messengers on horseback.

Virginia's proposal was at once accepted by all the other colonies, and Committees of Correspondence were created. Communications had at last been formed. Information and ideas could now be exchanged, and a common action decided upon.

The Committees of Correspondence were Jefferson's first important political act, and their effect was far reaching. They constituted the very first step in uniting the colonies, a step which in time led to the joining of the thirteen states into one nation. The year was 1773, and Jefferson was just thirty years old.

Jefferson now went home to Monticello, but during the summer months which followed two sorrows clouded his life.

John Wayles, his father-in-law, died. He had been a very wealthy man, owner of a number of plantations. Mrs. Jefferson now inherited 135 slaves and 40,000 acres including the now famous Natural Bridge which was ever to be a wonder and joy to Jefferson. This inheritance was encumbered with excessive debts incurred by John Wayles, but even so, after all had been settled what remained, Jefferson said, "doubled the ease" of their circumstance. At that time Jefferson's personal income was already very large for the time, being 3,000 dollars from his law practice and 2,000 dollars from his plantation of 5,000 acres and fifty-three slaves.

The second sorrow that summer was the sudden loss of Dabney Carr. He came down with a fever and died within a few days, at the age of twenty-nine, leaving Martha and six children.

Jefferson was away at the time, and Dabney Carr was buried at Shadwell. When he returned he immediately brought his sister and her children to live at Monticello with his family—children were ever to be his delight. And he remembered the pledge which he and Dabney had made when they were boys many years before, a pledge that they would someday be buried side by side on the "little mountain." So he brought Dabney Carr's body from its burial place at Shadwell and interred it at Monticello beneath the great oak where they used to sit and share their boyhood dreams of the future. This marked the beginning of the family graveyard at Monticello.

The Committees of Correspondence had not been organized one minute too soon, for in December of that same year of 1773 another struggle arose between England and her American colonies. Five years before, when Parliament had repealed the Townshend Act, it had retained the tax on tea. Few people besides Jefferson had foreseen the inherent danger. But now it became apparent to all.

To protest this unfair and heavy tax on tea, a group of Boston patriots, disguised as Indians, boarded three tea ships in the dead of night and dumped 342 chests of tea into the harbor.

The news of the "Boston Tea Party" traveled quickly to all the colonies by means of the Committees of Correspondence. The daring deed gave courage to others: Charleston merchants refused to accept a cargo of tea, in New York some "Indians" also held a "tea party," and in Annapolis a ship loaded with tea was destroyed by fire.

Because of the Committees of Correspondence the colonies were at last acting together, and the strength of their united front was immediately felt. The King accepted the challenge; Parliament passed a law, the Boston Port Bill, to go into effect on June 1, 1774, closing the port of Boston to all further trade. British troops were sent across the Atlantic to enforce this edict.

The House of Burgesses was aroused at the action taken by the King against Boston. Once more its members argued and debated about the best means of protest. Once more their efforts might have come to naught, if leadership in this matter had not been taken by those liberal and daring younger members, Jefferson, Patrick Henry, and the two Lees.

These men met in private as they had before. They felt that Virginia must give Massachusetts full support; Virginia must take a bold stand. And they devised a dramatic plan by which all Virginians would be awakened to the threat to their liberties contained in the "Boston Port Bill."

In order to bring the matter to the attention of

every community, no matter how small, they asked the House of Burgesses to appoint June 1 as a day of fasting and prayer, a day when all Virginians would implore God to "avert the heavy calamity which threatens destruction of our civil rights; and that the minds of His Majesty and his Parliament may be inspired from above with wisdom, moderation and justice . . ."

The House of Burgesses passed the bill. As might have been expected the royal governor again immediately dissolved the defiant House.

Once more the angry Burgesses gathered at the Raleigh Tavern. Denouncing the King's action in regard to Boston, they voted that "an attack on one colony should be considered as an attack on all." They also moved that the Virginia Committee of Correspondence should propose to the other colonies that a Continental Congress, made up of representatives from all the colonies, should be called to discuss the problems which beset them.

That same day at the Raleigh Tavern the rebellious Burgesses rightly decided that they could not hope to function effectively if the governor dissolved their House each time he disagreed with them, so they also voted to form a Virginia Congress which would be out of his reach, out of the reach of the English king. Since this congress would be illegal, it could not be recognized by the crown and would, therefore, be able to function in freedom.

The people of Virginia, of course, elected the same representatives to the Virginia Congress as they had elected to the House of Burgesses. Jefferson was chosen as representative from Albemarle County, and Patrick Henry was chosen to represent his county. And the people's choice from Fairfax County was George Washington.

The idea for a Continental Congress was immediately accepted by all the colonies. It was agreed that it should convene in Philadelphia in September.

Therefore, the first and main duty of the Virginia Congress, which convened on August 1 of that same year, was to choose the Virginia representatives to the Continental Congress. Jefferson was determined that those delegates should be bold and clear in their actions. To this end he began to prepare a draft of "instructions" that he hoped they would follow.

He wrote rapidly and with ease. He dipped into his vast storehouse of knowledge and recorded his ideas on history, government, colonies, and on the British Empire. He had very decided views on these questions, views that no one had yet expressed, and he was eager to give them circulation.

Jefferson considered himself an "American." His forefathers had come to America over 150 years before. Therefore, unlike many of the other people in the colonies who considered themselves Englishmen, he felt no loyalty toward England. And he did not agree with those Virginians, some of them his friends, who believed that England had a right to regulate commerce and impose taxation on the colonies.

Jefferson presented some new and revolutionary ideas in his "instructions." He held that all peoples had a right to leave the country where they had by chance been born, and establish new homes and new societies under their own laws completely independent of the land from which they came. He said that such had been the case with the people who settled the thirteen colonies, and he said that the English king had never given one shilling to the colonies nor shown any interest in them until they became commercially valuable to Great Britain. From that time on, year after year, the King had followed a policy of economics designed to reduce the colonies to slavery. To sight only one example of this he wrote that Americans were forbidden to manufacture goods from the iron they produced: it had to be shipped to England, then the finished product sent back to the colonies for sale at a high price.

Then Jefferson wrote on the subject of slavery. He hated slavery and wanted to free his slaves but was unable to do so because the Virginia colony had rigid laws outlawing such an act. During his first term in the House of Burgesses, when he was only twenty-six, he had introduced a bill to make it legal for slaveholders in Virginia to free their slaves if they so wished. The bill was defeated, but now he returned to the subject, as he was to return to it again and again during his life. In his "instructions" he said that the abolition of slavery was the desire of the colonies but that every attempt in this direction had been thwarted by England. Why? Because Parliament was protecting the economic interests of a few British slave traders in preference to the rights of the American colonies and the rights of human beings.

The draft of "instructions" continued in this outspoken way, listing one abuse after another. It concluded by stating that the British Parliament had no right to exercise authority over the colonies, that England and America were two different countries. Until now they had lived under one ruler by choice and that for the colonies to part from the mother country was "a natural right." He also said that the King had no right to send troops to American soil, for in the eyes of Americans they were foreign troops. And he boldly stated that "kings are the servants not the proprietors of the people."

These were strong thoughts, radical thoughts for those days. Jefferson was years ahead of his time. To deny the divine right of kings was treason. He knew this but he felt that he was correct and he was determined to present his draft. He was determined to speak not only for himself, not only for Virginia, but for all the American colonies.

However, at this crucial time Jefferson suffered one of the greatest disappointments of his long life. He was suddenly taken so seriously sick that he could not attend the Virginia Congress. He could not present his "instructions" in person. And he was not chosen as a delegate to the First Continental Congress in Philadelphia. Those chosen were his cousin Peyton Randolph, Richard Henry Lee, Edmund Pendleton, Patrick Henry, Benjamin Harrison, Richard Bland, and the tall, shy George Washington.

What should Jefferson do? He was determined to have his "instructions" read at the Virginia Congress. With this end in view he sent a copy to Patrick Henry and another copy to Peyton Randolph, chairman of the Congress.

Patrick Henry seems to have ignored this revolutionary document, but his cousin was much impressed by what the thirty-one-year-old Thomas Jefferson had written. He laid his copy of the "instructions" on the table at the Congress for all to see and later read it to a group of representatives who gathered in his home. Many were impressed by its contents, but it was far too bold, too extreme to be adopted by the Virginia Congress. So the Virginia representatives to the First Continental Congress were given, instead, mild and conciliatory instructions.

However, Jefferson's "draft of instructions" did not perish. A group of his admirers had it published in pamphlet form in Philadelphia under the title *Summary View of the Rights of British America*. It at once received wide attention and in a few weeks it ran through several editions. Most of the delegates from both north and south read it, and many admired the ideas it expressed. Its contents were discussed; its lines were quoted. Now all the delegates from all the colonies knew the name Thomas Jefferson. Although he was not a delegate, his presence was felt at the First Continental Congress.

In the months that followed, *Summary View* was read by others throughout the colonies, and Jefferson's ideas began to influence the political thinking of the time. His pen brought him fame everywhere. He was now a national figure.

His *Summary View* was even printed in England by supporters of the American cause. Edmund Burke, one of the leaders of this faction, used it in a speech before Parliament. As a result of this, the British government added the name, Thomas Jefferson, to its list of dangerous persons in the colonies agitating against the crown.

6

Penman of Democracy

THE FIRST CONTINENTAL CONGRESS convened in Philadelphia for seven weeks, and spent that entire time trying to find some way of making England mend her high-handed ways toward the colonies. The final result was a boycott and an embargo. The colonies agreed that after December, 1774, they would not import any more English goods. If this boycott failed them, the colonies agreed they would try an embargo; they would not send any American products to the mother country.

Considering the strained relations which existed between England and America these were rather mild and disappointing decisions. One important thing, however, resulted from this first Congress; the colonies, although they were still independent entities, had joined together and acted in a common cause. They were never again to be separated.

The colonies had acted as one, but England still refused to learn her lesson. She continued using her usual methods. Seeing this the colonies began to feel that war was inevitable. Each colony armed itself, forming Committees of Safety. The royal governor in each colony, learning of this, planned to remove all stores of arms and ammunition. The governor of the Virginia colony was so frightened that he turned the Palace on Gloucester Street into an armed fortress. Then suddenly in the spring of 1775, when the situation seemed grievous indeed, England sent each colonial government a copy of a document written by the Prime Minister and called *Lord North's Conciliatory Proposition*. Did this mean that England had at last come to her senses?

When Virginia's copy of this document arrived, the royal governor convened the House of Burgesses. Its members, the very same men who also belonged to the illegal Virginia Congress, obediently came, but many of them were dressed in military shirts and carried rifles. As usual they greeted the governor and pledged allegiance to the king. They then handed *Lord North's Proposition* over to Thomas Jefferson for consideration. Who among them was better versed in matters of justice and liberty? Who among them could appraise it more clearly?

Jefferson studied the document and reported back as quickly as possible. He held that Lord North's proposals were not conciliatory at all; that England still retained the right to tax, impose duties, and restrict trade between the colonies and other countries.

The House of Burgesses accepted Jefferson's report. It then stated that it was "honor bound" to the other colonies and would only answer Lord North together with them. And so England would have to wait until the next Continental Congress which was to be held in Philadelphia in June.

On this note of defiance the House of Burgesses closed its proceedings. The royal governor and his family, fearing for their lives, took refuge on a warship in the river. After this the House of Burgesses never convened again. The king's government in the colony of Virginia was no more.

The illegal Virginia Congress, or Virginia Convention, as it was now called, had chosen the same men as before to represent Virginia at the Second Continental Congress. There was, however, one slight change but this change proved very important to the cause of liberty. Due to the serious state of affairs in Williamsburg it was felt that Peyton Randolph might be needed in Virginia, so Thomas Jefferson was chosen as his alternate. In June of 1775, after reporting to the House of Burgesses on *Lord North's Proposition* Jefferson started out for Philadelphia to take Randolph's place at the Congress.

He traveled alone, driving in a carriage with two spare horses in tow. He was late. The Congress had already been in session for thirty days and so he was eager to make all possible speed. But the roads were so bad, and in some places the country was so wild and desolate that on two different occasions he lost his way. It took him ten days to cover the 300 miles from Williamsburg to Philadelphia.

At last, however, he reached his destination, and he rented rooms in the modest home of a cabinetmaker on Chestnut Street. On the next day, June 21, he took his seat at the Congress, which was convening in a brick building called Carpenter's Hall.

Jefferson was thirty-two years old at the time, next to the youngest member present, and he was only an alternate for Peyton Randolph. Yet his arrival created a stir. He was at once recognized as one of the originators of the Committees of Correspondence and as the author of that pamphlet, *Summary View*, which had caused so much comment and excitement during the previous Congress. Those who had known him only by name or through his writing now saw this tall young red-haired Virginia gentleman for the first time. They liked his quiet manner, frankness, and good will. He at once attracted friends, among them John Adams of Massachusetts and the distinguished seventy-one-year-old Benjamin Franklin.

Taking his place among the delegates, Jefferson found the Congress in a state of high excitement. Critical events had crowded one upon the other during the past months. In March Patrick Henry had delivered an impassioned speech before the Virginia Convention in Richmond, and the words he spoke that day, "Give me Liberty or give me Death," were still ringing throughout the colonies. In April Paul Revere had ridden through the countryside outside of Boston spreading the alarm that British troops were starting inland to take over the supply depot at Concord. A band of farmers had engaged these troops at the bridge in Lexington. American blood had been shed; the "shot heard around the world" had been fired. Then in May a group of Americans under Benedict Arnold and Ethan Allen had captured Fort Ticonderoga on Lake Champlain, complete with all its artillery and military supplies. In June the

Second Continental Congress had convened in Philadelphia and had lost no time in resolving that the colonies were in a state of war against England. And casting about for a leader for the "Continental" forces the Congress had unanimously appointed George Washington commander of the Continental Army. Two days later, before Washington could leave Philadelphia, the Battle of Bunker Hill occurred.

Liberty was now more than a word. It was something that had to be won. Many delegates who ten months before had found Jefferson's views as expressed in his *Summary* too strong now came around to his way of thinking. He was quickly placed on a number of committees, and since he was famous as a writer he was asked—along with John Dickinson, a conservative—to draw up a document justifying the action of the colonies. This paper was called *Causes of Taking up Arms*.

Toward the end of this session the representatives took up the question of *Lord North's Proposition*. Jefferson was placed on a committee with Benjamin Franklin, John Adams, and Richard Henry Lee to form a reply.

Jefferson had already written a reply to *Lord North's Proposition* for his fellow members in the now defunct House of Burgesses. It was so powerful and direct that after reading it Franklin, Adams, and Lee asked Jefferson to draft the report for their committee. And his draft, with very minor changes, was immediately accepted by the Continental Congress.

The American Revolution had found its voice: Thomas Jefferson.

Returning home to his beloved Monticello, Jefferson was faced with personal difficulties. Not only was his baby daughter, his second child, Jane, dying but his lovely wife and aged mother were also ill. It was a trying time. He was deeply depressed, and it was not until some weeks after the child's burial that his interests returned once more to the cause of the colonies. But he did not leave Monticello.

He worked on the Albermarle County Committee of Safety, of which he was head, and he collected money locally for the distressed citizens of Boston. After his mother's death in the spring of 1776 he went to Richmond, a little settlement west of Williamsburg where the Virginia Convention now held its sessions. There, he worked on a proposition to be later presented at the Continental Congress in Philadelphia. In this document Virginia instructed them to move that the Continental Congress should declare the "United Colonies free and independent States."

This was the moment that Thomas Jefferson, the "American," the believer in "independence" from England, had been working toward for so many years. Now with the resolution safely approved by the Virginia Convention, he rushed north to attend the Continental Congress which was still in session. This time he did not attend as a substitute for another representative. This time he attended the Congress as a duly chosen representative of the Virginia colony.

The Continental Congress was now meeting in the Pennsylvania State House. The members had read a pamphlet called *Common Sense*. Its author was Thomas Paine. He had arrived a year before from England and was a close friend of Benjamin Franklin. In *Common Sense* he explained why the colonies should become independent of the mother country. He went over the abuses of the king, just as Jefferson had done in his *Summary View*, but he did so in such simple direct language that everyone could understand.

Under the influence of *Common Sense*, the Congress had just resolved that in order to protect themselves from abuses perpetrated by England each colony should draw up a constitution declaring itself a self-governing state.

Even though the colonies were now at war with England, and even though they had just resolved to draw up constitutions declaring themselves self-governing states, the hopes for a reconciliation with England were still very strong. Many people were still loyal to England and asked only for reasonable and understanding treatment by the mother country. So when Richard Henry Lee rose and presented Virginia's resolution that the thirteen "United Colonies" should declare themselves "free and independent states" a storm of arguments arose.

The resolution was defended by three eloquent public speakers, Richard Henry Lee, John Adams, and Jefferson's old friend, George Wythe. But all their oratory could not sway the representatives of half the colonies: New York, New Jersey, Pennsylvania, Delaware, Maryland and South Carolina.

The fight raged for days and would perhaps have continued had it not been decided that to restore good will and sanity the subject should be shelved for three weeks.

However, the supporters of the independence movement did not give up hope. They felt that the other colonies would catch up with them. To be prepared, they persuaded the Congress to appoint a committee to draw up a declaration on the subject of independence. John Adams, Roger Sherman, Benjamin Franklin, Robert Livingston and Thomas Jefferson were chosen. Each came from a different colony, and each was a distinguished leader. A better cross-section of American patriotism could not have been found. And of all five men, Jefferson received the most votes and became the chairman.

It is recorded that at the first meeting the general tone of the declaration was discussed. Because Jefferson was so dedicated to the idea of independence and so capable, his fellow committee members asked him to undertake the momentous task. They asked him to write the document.

Jefferson wanted John Adams to do it, but Adams records that he said to Jefferson, "You can write ten times better than I can."

"Well," said Jefferson, "if you are decided I will do as well as I can."

Jefferson went to his rooms at once. He sat down in the parlor at a table upon which rested a unique little writing box that he had designed and had had made for him.

Here he sat and dipped his pen to give voice to his ideas.

Jefferson's original four-page draft of the Declaration of Independence is still preserved.

He wrote rapidly. He had no books or other reference material at hand. He tried to make his document an expression of the mind of America.

But it was more than that. Behind his pen, there was heat, there was inspiration, and there was creative imagination. His words were charged with honest indignation. Freedom was weighed in the scales of Justice. The "Rights of Man" were stated clearly and undeniably for all to see.

The Declaration of Independence was a short document. It opened with the concept that "all men are created equal," and that they are endowed "with certain inalienable rights" among which are the right to "Life, Liberty and the pursuit of Happiness." Jefferson then continued, reasoning logically. "That to secure these rights, Governments are instituted among Men"; that governments derive their power from the governed and that whenever a government jeopardizes the life, liberty and happiness of its people, it is the duty of the people to overthrow it and establish a new government which will assure these fundamental "Rights of Man."

The Declaration of Independence then listed the abuses perpetrated by England against its American colonies. In conclusion it stated that because of these excesses, because of this "Despotism," the colonies cast off the English government and declare themselves "Free and Independent States."

Such a burning declaration on the importance of the individual and his "inalienable rights," such a burning declaration that governments exist only for the people and not the people for the government, was startling and completely new in its time. It broke with the existing political concepts, left over from the feudal system, concepts which looked upon the common man as inferior and as the property of the chosen few, the property of aristocrats and kings who derived their power and wisdom directly from God himself.

Jefferson finished the first draft of the Declaration of Independence in two days, and he then showed it to his friends, John Adams and Benjamin Franklin. They approved of it, suggesting only some very minor changes, mostly in phrasing and in language.

The full committee then read and approved this version. On Friday, June 21, 1776, Jefferson presented his work to the proper authorities at the Continental Congress.

On July 1, Congress again took up the matter of Richard Henry Lee's resolution for independence. The three weeks of self-imposed silence was up; three weeks during which a great change had occurred in those colonies those had so strongly opposed independence. How had public opinion been so quickly swayed? It had come about this way. First, the stubborn position of the king had blocked all possible avenues of compromise; he would accept nothing short of complete surrender. Second, George Washington was a tremendously popular figure and his successes in the field had given the people hope. Finally Thomas Paine's stirring pamphlet, *Common Sense*, had penetrated into the most remote parts of every colony. Within a few weeks a hundred thousand copies were passing from hand to hand. Rich and poor were reading this brilliant essay. And rich and poor alike were converted to the cause of independence from England.

So on July 1, when Congress again took up the question of independence, opposition had all but vanished. The representatives were ready to consider Jefferson's draft of the Declaration of Independence. But Congress did not approve his work critically. Every line was studied and weighed. There were arguments, even debates.

John Adams and Benjamin Franklin vigorously defended every word of the original document. But in the end, in spite of their efforts, two main changes were made: the people of England were not to be held responsible for the unjust actions of their king, and slavery was not to be forbidden in America. Returning to a subject that was to haunt him to the end of his life, Jefferson had incorporated into his document a clause abolishing slavery. But South Carolina and Georgia wanted slavery to continue. And their position was supported by the delegates from a few northern states where there were some rich and powerful merchants who were engaged in this abhorrent traffic from Africa.

Jefferson was greatly distressed at seeing his document altered. But he sat silent, and Benjamin Franklin, the wise old philosopher, sensing how he was suffering, came and sat beside him and whispered amusing stories in his ear.

The debates on the Declaration of Independence lasted for almost two days, with John Adams defending Jefferson's work against all opponents right to the very end. The weather was pleasant. But the delegates were uncomfortable in their powdered wigs and knee breeches because the hall, being close to a livery stable, was filled with flies that buzzed about and bit through their silk stockings.

At length, on July 4, 1776, the debates were closed, the members of the Continental Congress voted to accept the Declaration of Independence as amended. Congress resolved to have it engrossed on parchment.

On August 2, 1776, the document was ready to receive the signatures of the members of the Continental Congress. John Hancock, a delegate from New York, was the first to come forward. He wrote in a large clear hand. The crown had a price upon his head for treason, and he said that he wanted his signature large and clear so that John Bull could read his name without using spectacles. Then followed the signatures of all the other delegates who were present.

As he signed, Benjamin Franklin is reported to have said something to the effect that "Now we must all hang together, or we shall all hang alone." It was a proud moment for George Wythe when he put his name beneath that of Thomas Jefferson.

7

Lawmaker

THOMAS JEFFERSON was re-elected to the next session of the Continental Congress, but he declined this honor. His wife was still ill, and did not want to stay in Philadelphia so far away from Monticello. During the last session he had been under the strain of constant worry about her. The mails were slow and not dependable, and he had awaited each post anxiously. Besides he had just been elected to the lower house of the legislature of the new state of Virginia, and he thought he could do more good in that capacity than as a member of the Continental Congress.

One must remember that although the thirteen colonies had declared their independence from England they were still not a nation; the idea of a United States of America had occurred to only a very few, such as Benjamin Franklin. They were just thirteen separate states, each with its own laws. Their only common bond was the Continental Congress and the Continental Army under George Washington, both of which had been formed solely to fight a common enemy, England. It was perfectly natural for Jefferson to feel that his duty lay in Virginia, in his state, in his "country."

Jefferson took his seat in the Virginia legislature determined to become the leader of a sweeping program of reform. He received immediate support from a large number of his fellow legislators. However his strongest support came from his old friends, George Wythe and George Mason.

Support also came from a young man, James Madison, who like Jefferson had been a student of Dr. James Maury.

During the three years that Jefferson served in the legislature he was given, together with Wythe and Pendleton, the task of revising all of Virginia's existing laws.

This was a task that Jefferson relished, and whenever the legislature was not in session he retired to the peace and happiness of Monticello to work on it. But he was not idle at other times. When the legislature was in session he also worked on a reform program. He introduced many bills, some mild but others shaking and revolutionary for their time. Among these were: a land bill, a slavery bill, and a bill for religious freedom.

The Virginia planters, many of whom were Tories or aristocrats still loyal to the King, rose up in protest against his land bill. They felt Jefferson was a traitor to his class, and they fought him with all their power and money. But their efforts failed. The need for change was too strong. After a long bitter struggle Jefferson came through victorious, and the vicious system of inherited power and wealth crashed to the ground.

During this session of the legislature, Jefferson also proposed a bill to curb the spread of slavery. He now realized that he could not abolish slavery in Virginia because it was too well established economically. The tobacco planters depended upon it. He thought the next best thing to do would be to limit slavery by prohibiting the further importation of slaves. And this time he was successful. His bill was passed, thus making Virginia the first state to have such a law.

These two bills all marked important breaks with the past and reached toward a democratic future. But the most important reform which Jefferson accomplished at this time and the one of which he was most proud was his bill for religious freedom.

Jefferson felt that a people could only enjoy true freedom and a democratic way of life if church and state were separate.

He also felt that people had a right to their own convictions and that this right should be respected. Many of the early settlers had come to America seeking religious freedom, and Jefferson maintained that no state religion should be imposed upon minority groups.

It was a long, hard battle. Fortunately Jefferson did not have to fight it alone. He had many friends who supported his idea, among them George Mason and James Madison, and after Jefferson left the legislature they carried his fight on to victory. Almost nine years later Jefferson's bill of religious freedom became law. The state of Virginia became the first state of the thirteen states and the first place in the western world where man could worship God or not, as he pleased and where he pleased, without fear or danger of persecution.

Complete religious freedom was now a reality in Virginia. Soon it was to become a reality for all states, for when the states finally became one nation the essence of Jefferson's bill was incorporated into the Constitution as the First Amendment in the Bill of Rights.

Until now Jefferson had been respected by most people. But with his support of the land reform bill and his ideas about slavery and freedom of religion, he was now a target for many.

8

Governor

PATRICK HENRY was the first governor of Virginia. When his term was ending leaders proposed Jefferson as next governor. But Jefferson was not too eager. He had devoted the last several years to the cause of freedom and democracy. He had given up his law practice and had been separated from his family for long periods of time. He was also much concerned about his wife's health. In 1777 she had given birth to a little boy who died when only a few days old and the next year given birth to a little girl named Mary. He was anxious to be with her at Monticello.

His friends were insistent; he finally agreed to run. His opponent was an old college friend and political associate, John Page. Although Jefferson was more distinguished, he only won by a narrow margin. John Page rolled up 61 votes to Jefferson's 67 votes.

Jefferson was thirty-six years old when he became governor of Virginia, and he served for two years. From his first day in office he was forced to center all his attention on the conduct of the war against England.

France had entered the American Revolution giving strong military aid to the colonies against her old enemy England. England, fearing that if the colonies won, France would then take possession of them, had increased her war efforts. The war had therefore spread into the south. The Carolinas were being devastated and Virginia was in danger of invasion.

The situation was critical, and Jefferson kept in close touch at all times with George Washington. He did everything he could to help the cause. He undertook the exchange of prisoners. He protested and took action against the English for the mistreatment of American soldiers, and he tried to keep Washington's army supplied with essentials. In one letter Washington wrote him that the troops were in desperate need of clothing, "especially of shoes, stockings, and linen."

At the same time, to prevent the English from invading Virginia Jefferson sent all the men and ammunition and supplies he could raise to General Gates, who was fighting the British under Cornwallis in the Carolinas. This was the intelligent and correct thing to do and was according to Washington's wishes, but the plan failed. General Gates was defeated, and Virginia then lay wide open to invasion.

From the very first, the State of Virginia had given so generously to the war effort that now, at this critical moment, she found herself defenseless. She had given the Continental Army so many horses and wagons that farming was very difficult and food scarce.

Week after week the people of Virginia waited for Cornwallis and his armies to swarm over their lands. But the Carolina Minute Men harassed his forces so seriously that he was delayed, and the first British attack against Virginia did not come from the land but from the sea. On December 23, 1780, a fleet of twenty-seven British ships sailed up the James River to Richmond.

Knowing this, the legislators fled, taking their families to safety and leaving Jefferson alone to handle the desperate situation. He was a man of great courage and so he did not falter. Sending Mrs. Jefferson with a new baby girl and little Martha and Mary to stay with relatives at nearby Tuckahoe, he immediately notified George Washington's headquarters, that the enemy was on the doorstep of the State Capitol. Then, mustering as many men as he could, he removed all war material from Richmond to a place of safety a few miles inland. By now Benedict Arnold and his troops had entered Richmond. From a distant hilltop Jefferson could see smoke rising from the town. The British had sacked all the buildings and had set fire to several homes and large warehouses.

However the British did not tarry long in Richmond, nor did they push inland.

The sacking of Richmond proved to be the opening attack of a much larger campaign. Virginia was now a battlefield, and the legislature meeting in devastated Richmond gave Jefferson dictatorial powers. Jefferson, the man of democracy who hated tyranny above all else, now wielded the power to arrest, to print money, to command the militia and to confiscate property including food, equipment and slaves.

These were dark days for Jefferson. He was not a military man and the duties cast upon him were distasteful, but he did not falter. He gave unsparingly of himself and he acted at all times with complete honesty and to the very best of his ability.

At last, in answer to his repeated calls for help, George Washington, who was also being hard pressed in the north, sent 1,200 light infantry to Virginia under the command of a young French major-general, the Marquis de Lafayette.

Lafayette's forces did not relieve the situation to any appreciable extent, and the legislature, seeking a safer place, moved to Charlottesville.

Scattered members of the legislature finally convened at a place called Staunton. They were deeply distressed by the brutal invasion of Virginia. Jefferson's second term as governor had expired, and a new governor had not been chosen to fill this office. Some of the legislators, under the tension of the time, heaped all the blame for the disastrous situation on Jefferson.

Jefferson's critics also asked what good was Jefferson's democracy if it could not meet the conditions of war and defend the land against enemies? They said that if self-government was worthless in times of crises then it was not worth having in times of peace.

In order to correct the evils which they said had been brought on by democracy they presented a bill calling for the creation of a dictatorship. One young representative, George Nicholas, suggested that an inquiry be made into Jefferson's actions, and in the days that followed a list of formal charges were actually drawn up.

Jefferson was shocked by these accusations. When he later learned that his enemies were talking of impeachment, he decided to retire forever from public life. He had always behaved in the best interests of his fellow men and his country. Washington and his commanding officers had expressed full satisfaction with his military actions. If he had failed it was not for lack of patriotism or personal sacrifice; his family had suffered during these days and his infant daughter had died. But he refused to surrender to the forces of reaction and autocracy. He decided to wage one more fight for democracy. He was determined to defeat his enemies' bill and see that a good man, a General Nelson, should be chosen as the next governor. He rallied his friends in the Legislature and elsewhere in Virginia and fought the monstrous measure to abolish the republican way of life and appoint a dictator. In the end he was victorious, and General Nelson was made governor. But it was only by a few votes that democracy won out during those critical days in Virginia.

Jefferson was now free of public office, but before he retired to Monticello he was determined to answer the charges which had been made against him. In order to do this he had to seek election in the Legislature; he could then be on the floor to hear the charges and defend his conduct. This he accomplished very easily for the people of Albermarle County gave him their full support; he was elected without one dissenting vote. When the state legislature next convened at Richmond, Jefferson was among its members.

However, the temper of the time was now changed. During the months which had elapsed since George Nicholas had made his charge, George Washington and his army had come into Virginia, engaged Cornwallis and defeated him at Yorktown. The Revolutionary War had ended. The colonies were victorious. When Thomas Jefferson rose in the Virginia Legislature and asked that the charges against him be read so that he could defend himself, not one voice was heard, least of all that of George Nicholas.

Jefferson was not satisfied with this silence. His honor had been attacked. He had a list of the accusations which a friend had managed to get for him, and he now read them aloud one by one, answering each in a clear and forthright manner. His defense completed, he sat down.

Another legislator immediately rose to offer a resolution. He asked that the ugly past be wiped out by thanking the former governor for his "impartial, upright" conduct and his high "ability" and "integrity." This resolution was unanimously passed by both houses. Jefferson was vindicated, and true to his word he went into retirement.

Many years later, recalling his dark hour, he wrote, "I stood arraigned for treason of the heart and not merely weakness of the mind," and he said that these injuries "had inflicted a wound on my spirit" which would endure until death.

9

Monticello

During the first few months of his retirement, Monticello provided Jefferson with the peace and tranquillity which he needed. He lived the life of a gentleman farmer.

He worked on plans for improving Monticello and its gardens, even designing furniture for its beautiful rooms. He designed, built and installed a compass on the living-room ceiling which, connected to a weather vane upon the roof, allowed him to know the direction of the wind at all times of the day or night. He also designed and installed a revolving door, with shelves which served as a buffet between the dining room and pantry. Another of his inventions was a double door of glass operated by a hidden system of ropes and weights that opened at the lightest touch on the handle.

For his personal use he designed such conveniences as a revolving armchair with a detachable

Monticello, which Jefferson designed himself, was built on land inherited from his father. Today it serves as a museum and monument to its creator.

footrest and writing board, and a worktable at which he could either stand or sit. It had telescopic legs, thus making it possible to adjust it to any desired height, or to cause the top to tilt forward for easier use when writing or drawing.

    It was during these same first months of retirement that Jefferson worked on a project that delighted him. France, being an ally of the colonies, was interested in receiving detailed reports from each state telling of its plants and animals, terrain and weather, and social and economic life.

    Jefferson had been invited to write the report on Virginia. No man was better equipped for this task, and no project could have pleased him more. Had he not since early boyhood roamed the forests and fields? Had he not lived in the rich

Tidewater lands and in the Up Country and later in gay Williamsburg and then Richmond? Had he not always kept notebooks of the details of the life around him, when the fruit trees blossomed each spring, how much rain fell, what the temperature was each day and a multitude of other such things?

So he sat down happily to record what he knew about Virginia. He wrote fascinating cameos on the geography, history and manners of his state. Since Virginia stretched far to the west he wrote about the Mississippi and Ohio rivers as well as the Appalachians and the Blue Ridge Mountains and the seacoast.

He recorded everything he knew about Virginia's beasts, fish and birds, plants and minerals. He wrote on farming, slavery, laws, commerce, Indian tribes and a hundred other subjects. He wrote from his deep love of nature and from his insatiable interest in life. When his *Notes on Virginia* was finished he had written a small encyclopedia, which remains to this day a most valuable historical record of the time.

Jefferson's months of retirement were happy months for him and his family, but his friends in Richmond and Philadelphia were much distressed by his absence. They had been shocked by the accusations brought against him and had rallied to his support, but after he had received a vote of confidence from the Virginia Legislature and particularly since young George Nicholas had published a letter of apology saying that his accusations were unfounded, they felt that Jefferson's continued retirement was nothing more than "bearing a grudge." Many of them wrote him stating their opinion very frankly. They said that his behavior was not worthy of a man of his stature. They pointed out that in politics everyone was open to criticism and they said that his help and guidance were essential to the survival of the young country.

His devoted disciple, James Madison, and his friend the twenty-three year old James Monroe, were especially upset by Jefferson's attitude. When James Monroe heard that he had declined a summons to return to Congress, he wrote Jefferson a very strong letter condemning his selfish behavior. He pointed out that Jefferson frequently had been elected to office "in times of less difficulty and danger than the present," but now, in the most critical period for the Thirteen States, when he was called to serve the public he had declined!

However, Jefferson had been so deeply hurt that he could not forget what had happened. He explained to his friends that being accused by the ignorant and uninformed was one thing, but to be unjustly accused by those who had worked closely with him and had known his purpose was more than he could endure. So he continued his retirement at Monticello. Then a great tragedy occurred in his life and all was changed.

In the spring of 1782 his lovely, delicate wife gave birth to their sixth child, a little girl, Lucy Elizabeth. Following this Mrs. Jefferson became very ill. She lay in bed week after week and although she was carefully nursed by her sister, Mrs. Eppes, and Jefferson's sister, Mrs. Dabney Carr, her strength ebbed each day.

Jefferson barely left her bedside and when, after four long months, death finally came he was so crushed with grief that he went to his room and refused to leave it.

Jefferson's friends in Philadelphia, learning of the great change which had occurred in his life, immediately decided to call him back into public service.

Now that the Revolution was over there was the problem of peace. They felt that the author of the Declaration of Independence should be one of the signers of the peace treaty. Congress unanimously elected Thomas Jefferson as a special minister to go to Paris and join Benjamin Franklin, John Adams, Henry Laurens, and John Jay in the negotiations with England. This time Jefferson did not disappoint his friends. He agreed to return to the political scene and serve his countrymen once more.

Ever since the days when Jefferson had been a student at William and Mary and had met Dr. Small and Governor Fauquier, he had dreamed of going to Europe. Through the years since the formation of the First Continental Congress he had been asked on two separate occasions to represent the colonies abroad but he had never before been in a position to accept. Now he was free to go.

He decided to take Martha with him. Providing for his sister and her six children, and leaving four-year-old Mary and the baby, Lucy, with their aunt Mrs. Eppes, he started out at once.

Arriving in Baltimore, however, he met with disappointment; he learned that the French man-of-war, the *Romulus*, on which he was to sail was icebound in the harbor. While awaiting a thaw, he went on to Philadelphia where he put Martha in school and spent his time studying the official papers and records related to his mission abroad.

Then at the end of January, 1783, he learned that the *Romulus* still could not sail because seven British ships were blockading the harbor waiting to capture her. England and France were at war because France had helped the colonies in the Revolution. So there was another long delay. Then the news came that the terms of peace had been drawn up without him by Franklin, Adams, Laurens, and Jay and had been accepted by England. So his journey became unnecessary, he was thanked by Congress for his willingness to undertake the mission and released.

Disappointed once more in his hopes of seeing France, he left Martha in school in Philadelphia and returned to the loneliness of Monticello. But he did not have time to brood or go into retirement, for almost immediately he received the news that he had been elected as delegate from Virginia to the Congress, which would convene this time in Annapolis in the fall of that same year.

Jefferson played a very active role in the Congress of 1783–84. He was appointed to several important committees, and within six months he had drafted over thirty state papers that have become building blocks of American democracy. The principles established by these acts helped greatly to bridge over that uncertain period in the formation of the United States of America, that critical period which lay between the end of the

Revolution and the welding together of the thirteen states into one nation under a constitution.

One of the important and unifying projects on which he worked during this session of Congress was the establishment of a uniform money system. Until that time all had been confusion; each state had had its own money system, and English, Dutch, French, and Spanish coins as well as tobacco were used for exchange.

Most of the delegates thought that the colonies should adopt the British system, but Jefferson and a few others were much opposed to this. They very rightly said that the British system was complicated and confusing; that it was not sensible for a new country to accept the mistakes of the past when it had the opportunity of starting anew. When Gouverneur Morris suggested the simple decimal system, Jefferson immediately supported him. He at once saw the practicality and wisdom of this system and gave it his full support, helping to work out certain problems that arose and insisting on keeping it simple and clear. Thus the dollar became our money unit.

The second important contribution which Jefferson made at this session of Congress was his plan for the future development of the Northwest

Territory which Virginia had ceded to the Confederation of Thirteen States, as they were now called.

About two and a half years before, back in 1781, while the Revolutionary War was still being waged, the Thirteen States had taken an important step toward uniting as one nation; they had adopted what they called "Articles of Confederation." Under these "Articles" the individual states retained almost complete self-government; they were like thirteen separate nations, each with the power to coin money, establish taxes and raise armies. However, they were joined together as one nation by Congress, whose purpose was to handle all matters national and international, to appoint ministers to foreign countries and to administer the Northwest Territory, that great area made up of the western lands once owned by Virginia and ceded by her to Congress for the mutual benefit of all.

Being a man of great vision, Jefferson presented a plan for the Northwest Territory which projected far into the future. He believed in the Confederation and he wanted to see it strengthened and enlarged. He proposed that the inhabitants of the Northwest Territory be allowed to create a temporary government under which to live until its population warranted that it be broken up into several states. The only requisites should be that both the territorial government and the subsequent state governments be republican or democratic in character, that no person with a hereditary title be given citizenship, and that after 1800 slavery be prohibited in this area.

This plan was immediately adopted by Congress, but with two changes that destroyed its meaning for Jefferson: the sections concerning hereditary titles and slavery were voided. The clause prohibiting slavery was defeated by only one vote. Jefferson was disappointed by this; he hated slavery, and, on moral grounds, he wanted to see it abolished.

10

Ambassador to France

IN THE SPRING OF 1784, Congress appointed Thomas Jefferson as a special minister to France to help John Adams and Benjamin Franklin, who were already abroad, to negotiate trade treaties with the different European countries. For the third time the promise of a visit to Europe shown brightly, but this time it was to be realized. Jefferson was free of pressing family responsibilities. His two youngest daughters were still with their aunt, and there was no ice in the harbor and no warships lying in wait. So Jefferson and twelve-year-old Martha sailed from Boston in July. "The sea was as calm as a river," wrote young Martha to a friend. It was, in fact so quiet that for three days the ship was becalmed off the Banks of Newfoundland and the crew went cod-fishing. In spite of this delay the crossing took only nineteen days—a very swift crossing for those days, before the invention of the steam engine, when ships depended solely upon sails.

Arriving in Paris, Jefferson lost no time in getting settled. He rented a beautiful home and through the kindness of his friend the Marquis de Lafayette, enrolled Martha in the city's finest private school, a convent called Panthemont. Having accomplished this he then turned to his mission. He reported to his old friend, the aging Benjamin Franklin, who was the ambassador to France and with whom he and John Adams were to collaborate in drawing up the trade treaties.

These three friends met regularly at the American Embassy, which Franklin had established on the road to Versailles, but their work was far from simple. To negotiate trade treaties with countries who knew little and cared little about the young republic across the wide Atlantic took much patience. Although they worked very hard, their efforts brought few results.

This was certainly not a very promising start for Jefferson, and soon he was left to deal with this problem all alone. John Adams was appointed ambassador to England, Franklin was relieved of his post, and Jefferson was named ambassador to France in his stead.

Benjamin Franklin had been as greatly admired and loved in Paris as he was loved and admired by his own countrymen. His absence would leave a void which Thomas Jefferson felt he could not fill. When someone said to Jefferson that he had heard that he was to replace Benjamin Franklin, Jefferson replied, "I am to succeed him; no one can replace him."

Now that Thomas Jefferson was ambassador, he moved into a more elegant home, not far from Franklin's old embassy on the road to Versailles. He bought himself a carriage and two horses, hired servants, and did all necessary to make his embassy as dignified and elegant as those of the other foreign ambassadors residing in Paris.

Doing this was of course very costly, and his salary would not cover the expense. However, Jefferson was determined that his country should be as well represented as the other countries and so he made up the difference from his personal funds.

Jefferson served as ambassador to France for a little over five years, and while his diplomatic duties were few they were nonetheless difficult. The Thirteen States had used up their small treasuries to wage the Revolution and they had not yet regained enough financial strength to pay back the debts which they owed the French government and private French concerns. Even the

French officers who had fought under Lafayette had not yet been fully paid. As a result Jefferson was constantly besieged by creditors.

But he did not just make excuses and beg for time. He believed firmly in the future of the Thirteen Confederated States and so he worked without rest to negotiate trade agreements that would give America the financial footing with Europe which she so sorely needed. His hopefulness inspired confidence in the new land. So alone and unaided he finally managed to conclude trade agreements with France, Prussia and several other European countries. These were the very first commercial agreements made by America and they paved the way for those ambassadors who followed Jefferson. In time all the debts owed the French were paid.

This was a great victory for the Thirteen States, but Jefferson's faith in America extended far beyond such direct money matters. Only a few years before France had lost New Orleans and Louisiana to Spain and so Jefferson kept in constant touch with the Spanish Court regarding American navigation rights on the Mississippi River. He tried to have New Orleans declared a free port. He had the vision to see that the Thirteen States would grow and expand; the Northwest Territory would in time become several new states. So he insisted that American ships must be free to sail on the Mississippi although all the lands to the west then belonged to Spain.

Jefferson worked faithfully in his capacity as ambassador, but he still found time to follow some of his personal interests. He read every French publication he could find, also publications from England and Holland as well as those sent to him from home. He arranged for the renowned French sculptor, Houdon, to go to America and make a life-size statute of General George Washington. He worked with a clockmaker on devising standard and interchangeable parts for watches and clocks, something which until then had been unknown. With his deep love for farming, he developed a new plow for which he was awarded a gold medal by the French Agricultural Society. But what pleased him most were the hours he spent on his "delight," architecture. The state of Virginia had written asking him to design the Capitol building for Richmond. So he spent many happy hours over his drafting board, modeling his work after a Roman temple in Nîmes, France, and his finished building, with very few changes, still stands today.

The French monarchy was firmly entrenched when Jefferson arrived in Paris during the summer of 1784. When he left France to return to America, five years later, the Bastille had fallen and the French Revolution was well under way. Jefferson knew that the French Revolution was to a measure inspired by what had happened in America. To a friend he wrote, "The American war . . . awakened the thinking part of this nation in general from the sleep of despotism in which they were sunk."

It was of course known in France that Jefferson was a specialist in such things as freedom and the rights of man; the Declaration of Independence was so widely read and had such a deep influence on the thinking of the French people that Louis XVI had outlawed it. Jefferson was asked by some of the French patriots to help in the drafting of a new constitution for France, but he knew if he gave aid in this he would compromise his diplomatic position and destroy his usefulness to his own country, so he excused himself.

However, his sympathies were definitely on the side of the French people. He felt they were taxed beyond human endurance, that they were "ground to a powder" by "monstrous abuses" and that the revolution was necessary to lift them out of this mire. He also felt that the Queen, Marie Antoinette, was an evil influence and he later recorded, "I have ever believed, that had there been no Queen, there would have been no Revolution."

While Jefferson's position as American Ambassador did not allow him to take an active part in French politics, he did nevertheless suggest that the King of France issue a Charter of Rights to the people. Such a charter he felt would avoid the terror and bloodshed of Revolution, but the king had poor judgment and was married to a queen who would allow no compromise with the people of France, and Jefferson's idea was rejected.

Day by day he saw the monarchy of France slowly crumbling, and growing weaker.

Then on the 14th of July, 1789, came the fall of the Bastille. Jefferson described how a few days later he saw the King come to Paris in his carriage protected by loyal troops. He described the scene as follows, "About sixty thousand citizens, of all forms and conditions, armed with the conquest of the Bastille [and with] pistols, swords, pikes, pruning-hooks, scythes, etc., lined the streets through which the procession passed." And he has recorded that he heard the people cry out, "Long live the nation!" But not one voice calling out the familiar, "Long live the King!"

During these same troublesome years which heralded in the French Revolution, things of great importance were also taking place in America. The thirteen states which in 1781 had adopted the Articles of Confederation were taking the final step which was to bind them together as one nation, the United States of America.

The states had decided to form a federal government and to draw up and adopt a constitution. Jefferson longed to be in Philadelphia to take part in the proceedings of the Constitutional Convention which was convening in that city. But since this was impossible he was forced to wait patiently and to hope for good results.

However, when he finally received a copy of the proposed Constitution of the United States, his disappointment was so keen that he could no longer contain himself. Although he liked the document in many ways he was quite angry that a Bill of Rights, guaranteeing the people equality and freedom, had been omitted. So he wrote letter after letter to his friends back home expressing his strong feelings on this crucial point.

Writing to Madison he urged him to have the proposed Constitution amended to include a Bill of Rights guaranteeing "religious freedom, freedom of the press and trial by jury." He said that the people were entitled to these guarantees and that no just government should refuse them. He wrote the same to George Washington. To other friends he suggested that the ratification of the Constitution be held up until a Bill of Rights was incorporated into it. He was most concerned about this important provision. He kept on writing letters, and he kept on insisting, and in the end it came about.

Although the proposed Constitution was adopted as it stood, Jefferson's devoted friend and disciple, James Madison, saw to it that Jefferson's wishes became a reality. During the very first days of the first Congress of the United States, he proposed the adoption of ten amendments, the ten first amendments to our Constitution. These amendments are our Bill of Rights.

Jefferson loved France and the French people but after several years of living abroad he began to long for America. During his stay he had suffered another great loss. Little Lucy Elizabeth had died of whooping cough back in Virginia. This had filled him with anxiety for his beloved eight-year-old Mary and he had immediately arranged for her to come to Paris. But even though he and Martha and Mary were now together, he began to dream of returning to Monticello. He wrote to his two close friends, Madison and Monroe, suggesting that they settle and build homes near Monticello. If they would only do this, he said, ''I shall believe that life still has some happiness in store for me. Agreeable society is the first essential in constituting happiness, and, of course, the value of our existence." So he asked for a leave of absence.

With the Thirteen States in the throes of forming a new government, affairs were so crowded at home that he was forced to wait. Besides the adoption of the Constitution and the formation of the Legislative and Judicial bodies, the country had to elect a president and vice president and provide for a national capital.

In time George Washington was unanimously chosen as first President of the United States with John Adams as Vice President, and New York City was designated as the capital of the new nation.

All these things took time to accomplish, so Jefferson had to wait a full year before permission for a six months' leave was granted. Five full years after he had arrived in Paris, he and his young daughters Martha and Mary began to pack for their happy trip home.

At last in October 1789, after many delays due to bad weather, their ship set sail carrying not only its crew and passengers but the Jeffersons' luggage as well. This, as might have been expected, included some unusual things, such as plants, shepherd dogs and innumerable crates of French furniture, paintings, mirrors and chandeliers for Monticello.

After twenty-six days of smooth sailing Jefferson and his two daughters once more set foot on American soil. This soil was the same that Jefferson had left five years before. It was the same, and yet somehow it was different. It was now the United States of America, the only land in the world at that time where men could enjoy true freedom—personal, political and religious. It was a land which, due largely to the work and vision of Thomas Jefferson, was to become the model of democracy and right everywhere on our earth.

Jefferson planned to spend his six months' leave at Monticello and then return to his post in France. He thought that the French Revolution would be over by the end of 1790 and that he could then hand over his affairs to a new American ambassador and retire from politics. He dreamed of returning to Monticello.

However, the very first American newspapers which he opened when his ship landed at Norfolk, Virginia, should have dispelled this fantasy. He read that President George Washington had just nominated him to the newly created post of

Secretary of State. "I made light of it," he later wrote to a friend, "supposing I had only to say 'no' and there would be an end to it."

With a happy heart he and his daughters journeyed from Norfolk to Monticello. Since there were no stages in those days, Jefferson borrowed horses and carriages from friends and relatives along the way. This was the custom of the time. Everywhere, he and his two girls were entertained with the greatest warmth. In fact, so generous was this Virginia hospitality that it took them a full month to travel the 150 odd miles to Monticello, where they finally arrived two days before Christmas.

Martha, who was then seventeen, left a description of this joyous arrival. When their carriage was four miles away the slaves already knew of their approach and they gathered at the foot of the "little mountain." Then as the carriage drew close they crowded around, unhitched the horses and shouted with joy as they drew it up the long hill to Monticello.

"When the door of the carriage was opened," Martha recorded, "they received him in their arms and bore him to the house, crowding around and kissing his hands and feet—some blubbering and crying—others laughing."

No homecoming could have been more joyous.

11

Secretary of State

WHILE JEFFERSON DREAMED of completing his assignment as Ambassador to France and then retiring for good to Monticello, President Washington had other plans, and so it happened that Jefferson never again returned to Paris. Washington felt that Jefferson was needed in the newly formed government, and he persuaded James Madison to visit Monticello and urge Jefferson to join his cabinet.

There was also pressure from other friends and, when President Washington wrote Jefferson saying, "I know of no person, who in my judgment could better execute the duties" of Secretary of State, Jefferson finally accepted.

"It is not for an individual to choose his post," Jefferson wrote to Washington. "You are to marshal us as may best be for the public good. . . ." He asked only for a few months' time to put his personal affairs in order.

The most pressing of these personal problems was the marriage of Martha, to her second cousin Thomas Mann Randolph. They had known each other as children and a year or so before, when young Randolph had completed his education at the University of Edinburgh, he had visited them in Paris, and a romance had developed.

Jefferson was very pleased with his son-in-law and at once put him in charge of Monticello and his other plantations, which due to his long absence were not being run as efficiently as they should be. Then arranging for little twelve-year-old Mary to spend part of her time with Martha and her husband and part of her time with her aunt to whom she was much attached, he started out on the long trip to New York City to take up his government post.

Passing through Philadelphia, Jefferson of course went to visit his beloved and distinguished friend Benjamin Franklin, who was at that time eighty-four years old. He found Franklin ill in bed but eager to learn all about the French Revolution and how his many French friends were involved in this upheaval. He, too, seemed to feel that the idea of liberty in France had been inspired by the success of the American Revolution. "They served their apprenticeship in America," said Franklin.

It was a heartfelt and interesting visit; the two friends had so much to speak about and to share with each other, but it was also a sad visit for Benjamin Franklin and Thomas Jefferson. They who had done so much to establish America as a land of freedom were never to see each other again. Franklin died a month later.

George Washington had been President almost a year before Jefferson joined him in New York City and became the first Secretary of State.

Jefferson's salary was $3,500 a year. He tried to live as economically as possible yet his expenses were such that he had to supplement his earnings by $100 each month. This he paid out of his own pocket, thus continuing a practice which he had begun in France and which was eventually to lead him into very serious financial difficulties. He had in fact already begun to feel money problems, for while in France his plantations had become so run down and his income had fallen so low that in order to come to New York he had to borrow $2,000. "I am only a farmer," he wrote to the private bankers, and he offered some of his land as a bond for the loan at six per cent interest.

Having returned so recently from France where the principles of American democracy

After spending five years (1784–89) in France, Jefferson returned to the United States to serve as Secretary of State under President George Washington.

were believed in and spoken of with such fervor, Jefferson was shocked to find that the same was not so among the members of the United States government and the rich people of New York

City. He was shocked to find that here at home the battle for democracy had still not been won. Freedom and those ideals for which the American Revolution had been fought were now threatened, by suspicion, by reaction, by lack of faith.

Jefferson was deeply disturbed to find that the upper classes in New York were completely out of sympathy with the democratic spirit. They still firmly believed that only an aristocracy had a right to rule. They openly preferred a monarchy to a government by the people; they said that democracy could never endure. And they all condemned the French Revolution.

Jefferson often found himself alone defending the new order in France. His was also often the only voice raised in defense of democracy. "I found myself," he said, "for the most part the only advocate on the republican side of the question."

This was a very distressing situation to Jefferson, but what alarmed him much more was that many of the "Patriots" who had fought so staunchly with George Washington and some of the very men who had helped to frame the Constitution of the United States also held these opinions. John Jay, who was appointed Chief Justice of the Supreme Court, was most skeptical; he felt that democracy only led to bad government.

Fisher Ames and George Cabot, both members of Congress from Massachusetts, spoke openly against democracy. Gouverneur Morris believed that senators should be appointed to serve for life and that they should come only from the ranks of the rich and aristocratic. The patriotic John Adams from Boston, who was then serving as Vice President of the United States, even his friend Adams now had a deep distrust of democracy. He was convinced that men who preached about "liberty, equality and fraternity and the rights of man" were of low character and could be hired for a fee. He once wrote, "Remember democracy never lasts long. It soon wastes, exhausts and murders itself."

Members of Congress, the Chief Justice and the Vice President all lacked faith in the government of the United States. All these and one more—the brilliant young Secretary of the Treasury, Alexander Hamilton, opposed democracy. He became the spokesman of all those who felt as he did. He became the leader of the "Federalists"; those who felt that the people could not govern themselves and that the federal government should be very powerful with the state governments subservient to it.

This was the alarming and depressing situation which Jefferson found on his arrival in New York.

However he was not a man to surrender the ideals for which he had worked so ardently. He was not a man who would allow Hamilton and his supporters to go unchallenged, so, rallying a few friends to his side, he determined to fight Hamilton and the Federalists.

There ensued a bitter contest between these two men, two of the ablest men in America, a contest in which one defended an old order and the other insisted on a new order. It lasted for twelve long years, during which time the scales tipped one way and then the other.

It was during his first three months in New York that Jefferson became party to a political deal which he later regretted because he felt that the facts had not been honestly presented to him. He felt that the threat to the young country had been grossly exaggerated in order to win his support.

This deal concerned the choice of a site on the Potomac River as the new location for the capital of the United States and the Assumption Bill for establishing the credit of the United States. Strangely enough, Jefferson entered into this pact with his political enemy, Alexander Hamilton.

Now although Alexander Hamilton was a Federalist, he worked very hard as Secretary of the Treasury to establish a firm financial base for the new country. Since he believed in a strong central government he devised a plan which would weld the many states into one unit and make every citizen conscious of his duty to the federal government. He decided that the federal government should assume all the debts incurred by the states for fighting the Revolution and that it should tax every citizen in order to raise the necessary money to pay off this indebtedness. Paying off a common debt, he felt, would unite the people and make them conscious of their duty to the federal government as nothing else could.

Hamilton was probably right, but although he was a very honest man his plan had a great fault; it opened the way for speculators to get rich at the expense of the people. When this was pointed out to Hamilton he agreed that some dishonest people would benefit but that this could not be helped; he said that American credit must be established once and forever and that his plan was the only way of accomplishing this end.

Because the treasuries of the states had been so quickly depleted after the break with England, the men who fought in the Continental Army and the farmers and craftsmen who had supplied George Washington's troops with food, clothing and guns had been paid with promissory notes.

During the years that followed these notes dropped in value; they fell from one dollar to ten and fifteen cents and the farmers and craftsmen, thinking they would never be redeemed, were anxious to get rid of them.

Now the first point of Hamilton's financial plan, or the Funding Bill, was to tax the people in order to redeem these notes at full value. Certain unscrupulous men and members of Congress having advance notice of this, rushed through the country buying up the deflated notes from the innocent and uninformed farmers and craftsmen. Great fortunes were made overnight and the people everywhere, discovering what had happened, were so aroused that when Alexander Hamilton presented the second part of his financial plan, the Assumption Bill, it met with violent opposition.

Hamilton's Assumption Bill provided that the federal government would assume the war debts of the states and again tax the citizens everywhere in order to pay off this indebtedness.

Now the states with the largest debts were in the North and they therefore favored the bill. However, Virginia and several other southern states had worked very hard and already paid off most of their state war debts, so they thought it wrong that they should be taxed to pay the debts of Massachusetts and the other northern states. It was further pointed out that the Assumption Bill would again help the speculators who were mainly northerners and who were busily buying up state certificates.

In spite of this, the Senate which had many Federalist members in its midst, passed the bill. However when it came to the House of Representatives it was defeated by a small margin.

"This measure," said Jefferson, "produced the most bitter and angry contest ever known in Congress before or since the Union of the States."

It was at this critical moment that Alexander Hamilton sought the help of Thomas Jefferson.

Jefferson's own words tell the story. "Hamilton was in despair. As I was going to the President's one day, I met him in the street. He walked me backwards and forwards before the President's door for half an hour. . . . He observed that the members of the administration ought to act in concert; and though this question was not of my department, yet a common duty should make it a common concern; that the President was the center . . . and that all of us should rally around him. . . ." Hamilton also suggested "that the question having been lost by a small majority" an appeal by Jefferson to some of his southern friends "might affect a change in the vote, and the machine of government, now suspended, might be again set in motion."

He further suggested that since the southern states did not like having the nation's capital in New York City and since they wanted it moved to some spot on the boundary between the North and South, some deal might be arranged.

Recognizing the importance of establishing the credit of the United States and wishing at all cost to save the Union, Jefferson agreed to help Hamilton. He proposed that they have dinner the next day, and he also invited the two congressmen from Virginia.

A compromise was arranged, and the Union was saved. Hamilton promised to persuade northern congressmen to vote for a bill that would establish the capital of the United States on the Potomac River and the congressmen from Virginia promised to win support for Hamilton's Assumption Bill. The promises were kept. Hamilton's bill was passed and the South got the capital located on its border in a district which was not to exceed ten square miles.

It was also agreed at that time that while the new capital was being built, the government should be moved to Philadelphia. And so a few months later, in December, 1790, the United States Government moved.

The cleavage between the Federalists, led by the energetic and brilliant Alexander Hamilton, and those who followed Jefferson, or the anti-Federalists as they were now called, became more pronounced by the events of the French Revolution. The Federalists hated the Revolution. They favored the monarchy not alone for France but for every country in the world, while the anti-Federalists naturally wanted to see an end to kings and the adoption of democracy everywhere. So the chasm between these two main political forces in America became wider and deeper, and their differences became more intense with the publication of Thomas Paine's new pamphlet, *The Rights of Man*.

The fight for democracy was now out in the open. Hamilton and his Federalists struck out boldly. In their newspaper, the *Gazette of the United States*, they printed their opinion that democracy was only the road to anarchy, and the editor frankly said that he wanted to see the United States transformed into a monarchy.

In answer to this Jefferson and his friends, the anti-Federalists, in the summer of 1791 began to publish the *National Gazette*. This little paper, printed twice a week, was one of the very first publications in America to voice the ideals of democracy and also champion the French Revolution.

During all this time the country was enjoying a wave of prosperity greater than it had ever known. This, together with the success of his financial policies, made the Secretary of the Treasury even bolder than he had been before. He now meddled openly in the affairs of the other government departments, especially in matters concerning the State Department's relations with England and France.

At length, Jefferson, who was ever quiet and soft spoken and who depended on reason and good sense, began to tire of the continual battles and wanted to resign. He spoke to President Washington about this on several occasions, but Washington would not hear of it.

Washington had the greatest respect for Thomas Jefferson. In fact, when his first four-year term was drawing to a close, he wanted Jefferson to succeed him as President and he spoke to James Madison concerning this matter. Madison, who knew Jefferson intimately, realized that such a thing was impossible. He answered that Jefferson was determined to retire from politics and that the Federalists would most certainly oppose the election of Jefferson.

These were dangerous times for the young republic. There were days when it all seemed hopeless, but President Washington never gave up. He was the one man in the whole country who had the respect of both contending factions, and he did all in his power to hold the government together.

Both Jefferson and Hamilton knew this, and each privately urged Washington to continue in office for a second term. Although Washington was sixty years old and in failing health, he accepted; but he appealed to Jefferson and Hamilton to heal their differences.

Jefferson and Hamilton were temperamentally opposed to each other. Their philosophies and ideas of government were opposite. To compromise with Hamilton, Jefferson would have had to surrender the very heart of his democratic ideals and his faith in the people. This he was unable to do.

So the feud continued into President Washington's second term, and once more Jefferson tried to resign. He told Washington that Hamilton's slanders against his character had to be refuted and that he could best make such a public defense as a private citizen.

But President Washington pointed out once more that he needed both Jefferson and Hamilton in his Cabinet. And he appealed to Jefferson's sense of patriotic duty. Monroe and Madison and other friends also pleaded with Jefferson; he must stay and fight to save the country from the Federalists. So Jefferson consented to serve for a while longer.

One result of this bitter feud should be noted. When the battle against Hamilton and the Federalists first began, Jefferson and his friends were known simply as anti-Federalists. Later, as the conflict continued and the anti-Federalists grew more organized, they began to call themselves "Republicans" in order to designate that they were loyal to the republican ideals as expressed in the Declaration of Independence and in the Constitution. Since their republican doctrine was also democratic, there were some who described themselves as "Democratic-Republicans." This term caught on and was soon simplified to plain "Democrat."

Because of heavy storms in the Atlantic during the winter of 1793 there had been no news from Europe for three months. Then in April the ships that arrived brought the news that all the kings of Europe had declared war against the newly established French Republic and that Louis XVI had been beheaded. To complicate affairs still further, Revolutionary France had declared war on England.

What position was America to take? Would our treaties of alliance and trade with the former monarchy of France be upheld? Would the new ambassador from the French government be received? Would England allow America to remain neutral?

Hamilton, who like many other Federalists, had put on mourning for the guillotined Louis XVI, advocated an immediate break with the new French government. He reasoned that since the treaties of alliance and commerce were signed by the king and since the king was now dead the agreements were no longer binding. Jefferson, who knew that the French Revolution was a necessary evil, that it was the only way in which a new social order could be established in France, defended the treaties. He said that the authority of a state stems from the people and not from the king. All rulers, he said, were temporary but the people were permanent. Therefore, the treaties between the United States and France were between the people of both nations; in signing these treaties the king only acted for the people of France.

President Washington upheld Jefferson's opinion in this matter, but he did not want to do anything to anger England. He was anxious to maintain a middle course, a neutral course. He did not want to provoke England with her mighty naval power for he knew that the health and prosperity of the United States depended on free shipping lanes.

And it must be said for Alexander Hamilton that although he sided with England, he was willing to agree with President Washington and Thomas Jefferson on this point.

While the majority of Americans remembered our Revolution and were still bitter against England, there were some who did not side with Revolutionary France. In conservative Philadelphia, as in New York, many had monarchist leanings, so Jefferson, the defender of the French Republic, was quite unpopular.

This, added to his feud with Hamilton, made his life very difficult. His temperament called for peace and quiet. Once again he appealed to President Washington to allow him to retire, but Washington still felt that Jefferson was needed and he prevailed upon him to remain in office until the end of the year. Finally, on the last day of 1793, the President accepted his resignation.

Now, once more, Jefferson declared that he was through with public life.

12

An Interlude of Retreat

JEFFERSON WAS SUPREMELY HAPPY to return to the life of a gentleman farmer. He needed the quiet of the country, and his plantations needed him.

His brief visits during the past ten years had hardly been sufficient to keep Popular Forest and his farms at Monticello in good running order. Even though his son-in-law had proved very capable there was much that still needed doing.

He wrote to Washington about a new idea of rotating his crops. "But it will take me from three to six years to get this plan under way." Time and patience, he said, were good rules for agriculture as well as for politics. He and Washington also discussed contour-plowing on hillsides. They were the very first farmers in the United States to use this method in order to preserve the top soil.

His travels in Europe had given Jefferson many new ideas. He remodeled his gardens and grounds. Following the European system, he planted fruit trees along the dividing lines of his large forty-acre fields. He also tore down some portions of his mansion so that he could rebuild them again in a more artistic manner—and he added a dome to the house of his dreams.

He built a flour mill, so that he and his neighbors could grind their own wheat. He set up a small factory where raw wool could be washed and made into yarn and then woven into cloth. After all he had over 150 slaves and their children to feed and clothe, and he was eager to make Monticello and his other plantations as self-supporting as possible.

Besides tobacco his farms provided meat, fruit, vegetables, grain, milk, butter and other provisions in liberal quantities. Those who worked for Jefferson always had plenty to eat, good shelter, good clothing, lots of firewood, tobacco to chew and smoke, and wine to drink.

Because of his fondness for experiment and his efforts to do things differently and in a more efficient way, Jefferson was ridiculed and called an impractical dreamer. Jefferson's only fault was that his ideas were far ahead of his time. Besides the "firsts" already mentioned, Jefferson was one of the first in America to encourage the use of farm machinery. He also imported sheep to improve the native breed, and he introduced to America numerous plants, such as melons and special nut trees.

When Jefferson first retired to Monticello, he avoided politics and read only one newspaper. He wrote Washington that he did not "suffer political things to enter" his mind. To John Adams he said, "I return to farming with an ardor . . . which has got the better entirely of my love of study. Instead of writing ten or twelve letters a day, which I have been in the habit of doing as a thing in course, I put off answering my letters now, farmerlike, till a rainy day." As time went on his resolve in these matters began to weaken, and so while supervising his plantations or tending his flowers and asparagus beds, his thoughts began to dwell on the state of the nation he loved so fervently and he began once more to share his thoughts on this subject by writing letters.

He could not resist writing about affairs that affected the nation, even to John Adams, the Federalist, although he again insisted that he was through with public life. "I have no ambition to govern men. It is a painful and thankless office."

Thomas Jefferson thought that he was through with politics, that he could retire to Monticello and enjoy his family and books. He felt that Monroe and Madison, his two devoted disciples, could carry on the fight against the Federalists or "monocrats," as he called those monarchists who were disrupting the peace of the country, but he was mistaken. He was much too intelligent, much too keen, much too concerned with his fellow men to be able to turn his back upon life.

Jefferson thought he could retire from the world, but he was also mistaken in this. He thought he could escape to Monticello but the world marched after him, right to his doorstep and invaded his home. Visitors came from Europe and from all over the United States.

When President Washington's second term of office was coming to an end, Jefferson's friends turned to him as their choice for the Democratic Presidential nominee. John Adams had become the candidate on the Federalist ticket, and they feared that he would win unless he was opposed by Jefferson. They felt that Jefferson was the only man who could get the support of some northerners as well as the votes of the southern planters and the western farmers.

Jefferson was not interested. He said that he had "no ambition to govern men; no passion which would lead me to delight to ride in a storm."

His friends feared that the Federalists would take over the government. Madison insisted that Jefferson had before him a "historical task" which was a duty, and so without his permission they put his name in nomination.

Jefferson did not protest. He felt that the people had the right "to marshal those whom they call into their service according to their fitness...."

Although he did not stir from Monticello to take part in the campaign, he rolled up an amazing number of votes. Of the four candidates he came in second. It was very close. The difference of only two electoral votes would have made him President.

While Jefferson did not win first place in this election, he did win the second place. Under the old system of elections the candidate who received the highest number of electoral votes became the President and he who received the next highest number became Vice President.

So John Adams, the Federalist, became President and Thomas Jefferson, the anti-Federalist or Democrat, became Vice President.

13

Vice President

JEFFERSON'S FIRST MOVE as Vice President was to try to re-establish genial relations with his old friend John Adams, even though they differed so widely in their political opinions. He wrote Madison that he was pleased that Adams had the highest position in the land. "He had always been my senior, from the commencement of our public life. . . . Mr. Adams and myself, were cordial friends from the beginning of the Revolution. Since our return from Europe, some little incidents have happened . . . His deviation from that line of politics on which we had been united has not made me less sensible of the rectitude of his heart. . . ." He wanted Madison to assure Adams of this fact so that it would work "to the harmony and good of the public service."

Jefferson's keen sense of patriotism and devotion to the people prompted him to put aside personal differences. John Adams did not have the same character and generosity. As President of the United States and leader of the Federalists he considered Jefferson an enemy and in the years that followed left him wholly uninformed about domestic and foreign proceedings. As a result, the administration of John Adams was marked by a cleavage and bitterness more intense than anything the country had ever known.

Adams and his Federalists took over the government planning to run it exactly as they wished, but Jefferson was determined to prevent this. He was in fact determined to destroy the anti-republican and monarchistic Federalists. He planned to attack them for every mistake they made. Since in those days the Vice Presidency was merely a position of honor, he had plenty of time to devote to this cause.

With their man, John Adams, sworn in as President of the United States the Federalists immediately launched their program. The young Republic of France was their first target.

Back in 1794, the United States had signed a conciliatory treaty with England, Jay's Treaty. This had angered France. She asked why the United States, whom she had helped during the Revolutionary War and with whom she had friendly treaties, should be courting the favors of her arch-enemy, England? America ignored this protest and so American-French relations had slowly deteriorated until the French were interfering with American shipping on the seas.

President Adams felt that something must be done at once. He sent three diplomats to negotiate with the French, but when they arrived in Paris they found Talleyrand in charge of all foreign affairs.

Talleyrand was a master of intrigue and political treachery, and he sent three of his agents, known as Mr. X, Mr. Y and Mr. Z, to negotiate with the Americans. These men, at first, pretended that they did not know what the Americans wanted. But if they wanted something then they must pay for it. Business was business. Even peace had its price: a loan to the French government and a personal gift to Talleyrand.

The American envoys were dumfounded. It was on this occasion that one of them replied in words that have since become famous. "Not a cent!" he cried. "Millions for defense, but not a cent for tribute."

Learning this, the people of America were filled with indignation. Then, even though the French Government denounced the XYZ Affair and swore it was innocent and that the three agents were unauthorized, the Federalists led by Alexander Hamilton declared that war was the only answer.

During the height of this war hysteria, Congress passed the Alien and Sedition Acts. These two laws were an attempt to choke off all political opposition to the Adams' administration and all criticism of the Federalist Party.

The Alien Act was directed primarily against a number of distinguished foreigners who had fled from Europe and were now living in America and actively working for Jefferson's Democratic Party. It gave the President power to order out of the United States all aliens whom he regarded as dangerous to the public peace or whom he suspected of "treasonable or secret" inclinations.

The Sedition Act on the other hand was aimed directly against Jefferson and all Americans who, like him, were against monarchy and for liberty and democracy here and abroad. Its purpose was to wipe out the Democratic Party. Free speech and other personal rights guaranteed in our Constitution were cast aside. The Sedition Act made it possible, among other things, for a judge to fine and imprison anyone whom he felt was bringing into disrepute the President, the Congress or the United States Government.

Jefferson knew that the Alien and Sedition Acts were unconstitutional; that they were in direct contradiction to the Bill of Rights. He also knew that they would lead to the complete ruin of the Federalist Party. Even though he was under close scrutiny by Federal agents and his mail was being opened, he wrote letters to his friends everywhere confirming his democratic beliefs and condemning the war-mongering of the Federalists and the Alien and Sedition Acts. Together with James Madison and a few other friends he drew up a manifesto declaring that the national government was created by the states; that it was a tool of the states and that its actions were liable to criticism and nullification by the states.

This manifesto was presented to the legislatures of both Virginia and Kentucky, two states that maintained that the Alien and Sedition Acts were unconstitutional. It was immediately passed by both of these houses, thus becoming the Virginia and Kentucky Resolutions.

It took the Presidential campaign of 1800 to deal the Federalists a death blow.

In this campaign, a most vicious and bitter campaign, John Adams and Thomas Jefferson again opposed each other.

The abuses of the Federalists, and the outrages the Alien and Sedition Acts turned the tide. Adams and his running mate Pinckney were defeated by Jefferson and his running mate Aaron Burr.

14

President

THE GOVERNMENT HAD MOVED from Philadelphia to its permanent home in Washington, D.C., in June of 1800. Thomas Jefferson was the first President to be inaugurated in the new national capital on the Potomac River.

At about noon President-elect Jefferson, dressed in green breeches, gray woolen stockings and a gray coat, walked the two blocks from his boardinghouse to the Capitol. Four years before, in Philadelphia, John Adams had driven to his inauguration in a carriage drawn by six horses, but Jefferson had a disdain for pomp and that vain display so dear to the hearts of the aristocrats; he preferred walking.

The Senate Chamber was crowded. Seeing Jefferson enter, everyone rose and remained standing until he had seated himself between Vice President Aaron Burr and a tall, thin black-haired man who was the newly appointed Chief Justice of the Supreme Court, John Marshall. Jefferson knew Marshall. They were distant cousins, Marshall being twelve years younger. Both were Virginians. Both had been pupils of that famous master of law George Wythe. Both had been members of the House of Burgesses. Both had been devoted friends of George Washington who had died about a year before. During the preceding four years while Jefferson served as Vice President to President Adams, Marshall had served Adams as Secretary of State.

Jefferson and Marshall had many things in common, but one thing separated them and this was important: their ideals. Marshall was leader of the Federalists in Virginia. This made him an enemy of Jeffersonian democracy.

Yet courtesy prevailed. The Chief Justice delivered the oath of office, and Jefferson repeated his solemn vow to uphold and defend the Constitution of the United States.

After taking the oath of office Jefferson unfolded a paper which he took from his pocket and in a clear voice, read his inaugural address. It was an appeal designed to end that bitter "contest of opinion" which had marked the last administration and campaign. It was a moving appeal for national unity and friendship.

A portrait by the artist Rembrandt Peal captures Jefferson at the beginning of his second term as president, in 1805. He was 62 years old.

He ended his address with a plea that the principles of freedom which had thus far guided the nation be held sacred because "The wisdom of our sages and the blood of our heroes have been devoted to their attainment." He assured the people of the land that he was opposed to intolerance and injustice and he said that he relied on their "good-will."

In a land torn by conflicting interests and two bitterly opposed political parties, this address, filled with good sense and moderation, did much to reduce the tension. It helped ease the way for a definite change in government. Now for the first time would begin a democratic administration over a land dedicated to democracy.

Jefferson brought democracy into the White House, but he did not live a life of austerity. He lived as he had always lived, with true Virginia hospitality. The White House was always filled with his family, friends and visitors. In order to make this possible he brought a dozen or more servants, including his French chef and his Irish coachman, from Monticello.

Jefferson also brought five of his horses, some of the finest in the country, from Monticello to Washington. His saddle horse, Wildaire, was a most beautiful creature and attracted a great deal of attention.

This was certainly a very pleasant way to live, but at the end of his first year in office Jefferson found that his salary was not enough. Since his plantations were still not paying as they should, he was again forced to borrow money to make up this deficit.

Jefferson's first job as President was to select the members of his Cabinet. James Madison became Secretary of State and he, together with the other Cabinet members, all worked in harmony. When, as often happened, their opinions differed Jefferson called upon them to confer; by "conversing and reasoning, so as to modify each other's ideas," they always arrived at a satisfactory result.

Jefferson also insisted that his cabinet members come to his study at the White House at any time of the day or night without appointment or ceremony. The nation's welfare came first.

President Jefferson's second most important task after selecting his cabinet was to erase the evils perpetrated by the Federalists during the last administration. He pardoned all those imprisoned by the Sedition Act. He then wrote personal letters of apology to many of these unfortunate people as well as to the victims of the Alien Act. Ashamed that the United States, a land dedicated to freedom, should have persecuted people as it had under these two vicious laws, he felt that it was his duty as President to make amends.

When Jefferson began his first term in office, the United States was enjoying a period of great prosperity and expansion. Pioneers were pushing westward toward the Mississippi, opening up fresh lands. Shops and factories were springing up in New England and other parts of the country, and it was Jefferson's desire to prevent anything from interfering with this growth.

He wanted the United States to steer clear of all European entanglements; he wanted to keep all European intriguers and aggressors out of America.

This was Jefferson's desire for America, and he felt that it could be realized because the Atlantic Ocean was wide enough to keep American isolated from European intrigues and European wars. But he was wrong. Napoleon, a young military and political genius, had seized control of the French Republic. Through military might he had made himself master of a great part of Europe.

When the French and Indian Wars ended in 1763, France lost all her possessions east of the Mississippi with the exception of the city of New Orleans. Shortly thereafter she lost this city and Louisiana, or all her lands west of the Mississippi, to Spain. During the forty years that had followed, first the thirteen colonies and then later the United States, were allowed by Spain to enjoy free navigation on the Mississippi. This was essential to the development of our western lands and to the growth of our country. Jefferson recognized this and when he was Ambassador to France he had cemented American relations with Spain in this regard. Napoleon demanded that Spain return New Orleans and Louisiana to France. Spain, helpless to do otherwise, had complied.

Jefferson searched for a solution to the terrible dilemma, and he came up with a plan. He asked Congress to grant him a secret appropriation of two million dollars to use as he thought best in negotiations with foreign nations. Congress, which was now predominately Democratic, complied.

Jefferson then appointed Monroe as special minister to France. He was to join the American Ambassador in Paris and attempt to purchase the city of New Orleans from France for the two million dollars provided by Congress. If need be they were to offer as much as ten million.

Monroe was thirty days crossing the Atlantic. But this delay proved to be an advantage, for during this time Napoleon received bad news; an army he had sent to quell a slave revolt in French Haiti was completely destroyed by fighting and fever.

Napoleon had planned on making this rich island the gateway to Louisiana but now without it and with the sea lanes controlled by England, he gave up the idea of a colonial venture in the New World. He turned his attention instead to Europe. Here was glory close at hand.

But he needed money. He worried about this and then suddenly he came up with a solution. Why not sell Louisiana?

And so, a few days before Monroe arrived in Paris, Napoleon's Prime Minister asked the American Ambassador if the United States would be interested in buying New Orleans and Louisiana and what price she would pay.

The ambassador was so startled and unprepared that he foolishly said that the United States was interested only in New Orleans.

Monroe fortunately arrived the next day. Now the Americans could act together.

Knowing that France was badly pressed and on the verge of war with England, they decided that a little delay might be to their advantage. They kept negotiations open for a full two weeks and then a bargain was struck. For 60,000,000 francs, or about $15,000,000, Napoleon sold New Orleans and the whole of Louisiana to the United States.

Jefferson was pleased at the news but he was not sure that the Constitution gave the President such powers as he had assumed. However, Congress raised no difficulties. The treaty was approved without delay lest Napoleon change his mind. The United States now stretched from the Atlantic to the Rockies, from the Gulf of Mexico to the Great Lakes and Canada.

New Orleans was a beautiful and prosperous city. This everyone knew, but what lay within the vast northern and western reaches of the Louisiana Territory was a mystery. Thomas Jefferson among others had long been anxious to learn about its secrets.

Many years before, when Jefferson was Ambassador to France, he had met the American explorer, John Ledyard, and had tried to interest him in crossing Russia and Siberia and then proceeding by boat to Canada from which he could enter the Northwest for exploration. This plan had not materialized but now that Louisiana belonged to the United States things were different. Jefferson got funds from Congress and adding money of his own he organized a party of exploration into this territory.

The expedition was headed by a young man of twenty-one, Meriwether Lewis, and an older man, William Clark, a woodsman and Indian fighter. Its other members numbered about twenty-five, among whom was an interpreter of Indian languages and his Indian wife.

Lewis was a neighbor of Jefferson's, living only a few miles from Monticello, and he had served the President as private secretary in the White House for two years. He was particularly well suited for this job of exploration since he was something of a scientist, a woodsman, and since he knew Jefferson well and understood exactly what he wanted.

The expedition left St. Louis in May, 1804, and returned two years later in the spring of 1806. President Jefferson could not have been more pleased with its work.

Lewis and Clark had gone up the Missouri River, crossed the Rockies, gone down the Columbia River and reached the Pacific Ocean. They returned with a detailed account of the whole vast territory. They had noted the character of the land, the rivers, plains and mountains. They had reported on the climate, vegetation, minerals and animals, and on the Indian tribes, their languages and customs. They also brought back specimens and fossils which Jefferson studied and displayed in the basement of the White House.

At the end of his first term as President,

Thomas Jefferson was the most popular man in America. He had encouraged national growth, reduced the public debt and doubled the territory of the United States. The country had never known greater prosperity, so he was unanimously nominated for re-election in 1804. He received 162 electoral votes to his opponent's fourteen votes.

Jefferson's first term had been years of triumph. His second term was filled with trouble. There was trouble with pirates, trouble at home and trouble with England.

The pirates of the Barbary States—that is, the pirates of Algiers, Morocco, Tripoli and Tunis—had for many years been collecting tribute from all shipping in the Mediterranean. England had been the first to pay the rulers of these countries so that her ships could pass freely from port to port. Other European countries had then been forced to do the same. As the United States grew and her commerce spread, she too became entangled in this evil web.

President Washington and President Adams had done nothing to put an end to this practice, but President Jefferson was of a different mind. Jefferson loved peace, but not peace at any price, and so now, when the Pasha of Tripoli increased his demands, Jefferson declared that America would pay no more tribute.

The Pasha at once declared war on the United States. Jefferson dispatched a force to the Mediterranean Sea.

By gallant fighting and a vigorous blockade, the war with Tripoli was over quickly and the Pasha agreed to respect American ships without the payment of tribute. The other Barbary States then followed suit.

It had been an unpleasant affair, but Jefferson's firm stand had brought the desired results. He had won respect for the American flag and our ships now enjoyed full freedom of the seas.

England and France under Napoleon were locked in deadly combat for the control of Europe, and had imposed blockades against each other. Each was suspicious that America was trading with the other, and this interfered with American shipping. French and English men-of-war hovered along our coast, stopping our ships, violating all the laws pertaining to neutrals. England was more aggressive because she had the greater navy. Needing all the seamen she could find, she not only searched our vessels for goods destined for France, but she took American sailors, and under the pretext that they were "runaway" British sailors, made them part of her navy!

This indignity infuriated Americans. Jefferson had once said, "Peace is our passion," but now this peace was being torn to tatters; the price for peace was dishonor.

Lacking a suitable navy, Jefferson was forced to seek another weapon. He decided upon an embargo. Once, before the outbreak of the Revolution, England had felt the sting of this economic weapon, and Jefferson hoped that it would work again. However he miscalculated. Cutting off our exports to England meant that our industries suffered. A business recession set in. Many business houses went bankrupt. The farmers, the factory workers and the small merchants suffered the most.

Widespread economic distress brought the Federalists back into power in the northern states, and they charged Jefferson with being a fraud and a dangerous man.

Some states even questioned the right of the federal government to impose an embargo, and they threatened to secede. President Jefferson was forced to sign a bill repealing the embargo on which he had placed so much faith.

Jefferson had made a serious political and economic mistake and been forced to admit defeat, but his enemies were not satisfied. They continued their attacks. Jefferson was blamed for everything that went wrong. He became the target for criticism on all sides. In spite of all this he was still politically strong and with his second term drawing to a close, he named his disciple, James Monroe, as his successor.

15

The Sage of Monticello

THE DREAM OF RETIREMENT which Thomas Jefferson had cherished for so many years finally came true. He was sixty-six years old. He had served his country, and he was free to live at Monticello.

Jefferson loved his daughter, Martha, and her husband. He loved his grandchildren. He enjoyed the company of his numberless visitors, friends and strangers alike. But the day was not long enough for everything he wanted to do. He now found that he had little time for reading and he compared himself to his friend of long ago, Benjamin Franklin. He wrote, "Dr. Franklin used to say that when he was young and had time to read he had no books; and now when he had become old and had books, he had no time."

Family and friends occupied much of Jefferson's day, but it was his correspondence that absorbed most of his time. Many of his letters were long and revealed his vast knowledge and his philosophy of liberty. They are priceless records that have vastly enriched our historical heritage. But of all these letters, perhaps the most remarkable are those Jefferson exchanged with John Adams. Here two men of great learning and accomplishment reflect upon the events that brought America into freedom and greatness.

For eleven years, Thomas Jefferson and John Adams had not been on speaking terms. Still, during the years of their estrangement they had retained great respect for each other and now, thinking back over the past, they longed to be friends once more.

So John Adams wrote to a friend, "I always loved Jefferson, and still love him." To this same mutual friend, Benjamin Rush, who was also a signer of the Declaration of Independence, Jefferson wrote, "I wish . . . to express to Mr. Adams my unchanged affection for him."

Replying to Adams' first letter, which closed with the line "I salute you with unchanged affection and respect," Jefferson wrote, "A letter from you calls up recollections very dear to my heart. It carries me back to the times when, beset with difficulties and dangers, we were fellow-laborers in the same cause, struggling for what is most valuable to man, his right to self-government. Laboring always at the same oar . . . we knew not how, we rode through the storm with heart and hand, and made a happy port."

And so in 1812, a little over two years after Jefferson retired to Monticello, these two old friends were reconciled. Adams was seventy-seven, Jefferson was sixty-eight.

Many years before, in 1776, when Jefferson was a young man and a member of the Virginia General Assembly, he had presented a plan for free grammar school, high school and college education for the State of Virginia. This "visionary" plan had never been put through but Jefferson had not lost hope. He still believed firmly that freedom in the hands of educated men and women had a better chance to survive than freedom in the hands of ignorant people. Now that he was retired he drew up a second and improved plan for mass education for the state of Virginia and had it presented to the legislature through a friend who was a member of that body.

However his second education plan did not succeed any better than his first plan. It was considered the work of a dreamer and voted down. At this Jefferson observed that legislators were themselves ignorant and did not know "the important truths, that knowledge is power, that knowledge is safety, and that knowledge is happiness."

Although again his plan for free education had been rejected, he still did not surrender. He kept hammering away and finally the state legislature voted a sum of money for the free elementary education of the poor and another sum of money, a small amount, for the support of a state university.

The long-awaited breakthrough had occurred, and with this slim opening Jefferson set to work at once to build a school of higher learning to be known as the University of Virginia.

His whole heart was in the project. No details escaped him. He drew up the architectural plans, laid out the foundations, hired the workmen and showed the bricklayers how to lay the bricks. He even imported marble and sculptors from Italy. When funds ran low he raised more money so that the work could continue. There were no obstacles which he did not overcome.

Since the buildings under construction were not far from Monticello he visited them almost daily. On other days, from the terrace of his home, he watched the work in progress through his telescope.

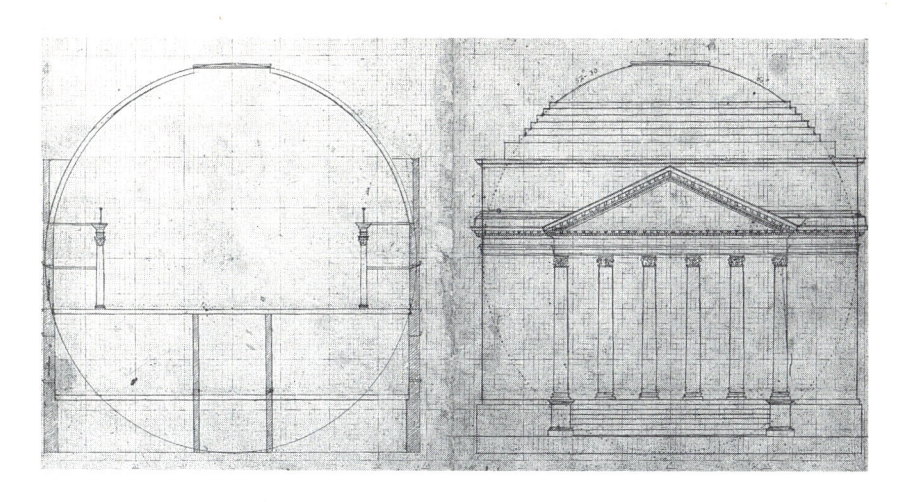

Jefferson conceived and designed the University of Virginia. His drawing (top) of the Rotunda was modeled after the Pantheon in Rome. The building itself was restored to his original design in 1976.

But the construction of the buildings and the landscaping of the campus were only part of Jefferson's plan for the University of Virginia. He chose the faculty, bringing most of his professors from Europe. When in 1825, after six years of hard but gratifying work, the University of Virginia finally opened with Jefferson as its Rector, it was the first modern college in America. Being a pioneer in education as he was in everything else, Thomas Jefferson had imported from Europe a system by which the students could choose to study the subjects they were most interested in and could specialize in certain fields. The University of Virginia was also the first nonsectarian college in the United States. Here all religious, as well as political beliefs were treated with complete equality, a thing unknown to education in those days.

Thomas Jefferson was eighty-two years old when the University of Virginia opened. This was one of the happiest moments of his life, but just the year before he had experienced another very happy occasion; his old friend the Marquis of Lafayette, then sixty-nine years of age, had come on a visit to the United States and had journeyed to Monticello to see him.

Lafayette and Jefferson had last seen each other thirty-five years before, in Paris, during the opening days of the French Revolution. However, during all those long years their hearts had been joined by their ideals of liberty.

Jefferson had written to Lafayette to hasten his visit to Monticello. "What a history we have to run over. . . ."

At last the day arrived. Lafayette's coach drew up to the edge of the lawn in front of Monticello. He was escorted by an American guard of honor of 120 mounted men with banners and trumpets. A crowd of about two hundred people had assembled to witness the scene.

As Lafayette got out of the carriage Jefferson started down the steps of the portico. They moved slowly toward each other for Jefferson now walked with difficulty and Lafayette was lame.

Jefferson's grandson, who was present, described what happened. "As they approached each other, their uncertain gait quickened itself into a shuffling run, and exclaiming, 'Ah, Jefferson!' 'Ah, Lafayette!' they burst into tears as they fell into each other's arms. Among the hundreds witnessing this scene there was not a dry eye."

The two aged men then entered the house. Lafayette remained at Monticello for several long weeks. So much did they have to say to each other. Together they had taken part in the history of their time and in the march toward Freedom.

Thomas Jefferson's last days should have been spent in peace, but they were not. Financial troubles beset him. After returning to Monticello his debts grew rapidly. Even though he sold much of his land, he was unable to stem the tide; the rest of his land and most of his slaves were attached by creditors.

At the age of eighty-three Jefferson was faced with the prospect of losing Monticello. To prevent this he offered his library, probably the best library in America, for sale, and Congress bought it. Thus Jefferson's library became the nucleus of our present Library of Congress.

But even this was not enough to save Monticello, and Jefferson applied to the State of Virginia for permission to sell off some of his land by lottery. Permission was granted; but it was not necessary for him to resort to this, for news of his distress had filtered out and offers of assistance came from many parts of the country. The hearts of the people were moved. They did not want to see Thomas Jefferson, the author of the Declaration of Independence, lose his home in his old age.

Meetings were held. New York City raised $8,500 dollars, Philadelphia $5,000, Baltimore $3,000. Other cities also donated. The total was $17,000.

These gifts from the people of the United States, the people, for whom Jefferson had always fought, filled him with joy. It was the greatest tribute he had ever received, and he recognized it for exactly what it was, "the pure and unsolicited offering of love."

In March of 1826, he wrote out his will. Monticello and what little land he still owned he left to Martha and her children. To James Madison he left his gold-mounted walking stick "as a token of the cordial and affectionate friendship which for nearly now a half century has united us in the same principles. . . ." The books he had collected since his library was sold to Congress he left to the University of Virginia. He remembered each of his grandchildren with a gold watch, and he gave his three personal slaves their freedom, ordering that each should receive a log cabin and the necessary tools to earn a living.

As summer drew near, Jefferson received an invitation from the citizens of Washington, D.C., to attend a Fourth of July celebration commemorating the signing of the Declaration of Independence, which was now fifty years old. But his health forced him to decline.

In his letter of regret, he summed up this period. "All eyes are opened, or opening, to the rights of man. . . . That the mass of mankind has not been born with saddles on their backs . . . These are grounds of hope for others."

It was now just fifty years since he had written the Declaration of Independence. In this half century he had seen America grow from a population of three million people to about ten million. He had seen thirteen separate colonies grow into twenty-four states. He had seen the land stretch from Florida to Canada and west to Oregon, and he felt certain that it would in time touch the Pacific Ocean. His dream of a government by the people had, in these years, been tried. It was no longer an experiment. Democracy was now the established way of life in the United States. And this democracy included religious freedom and the rights of man. He was content. His work was done.

The end came to him gently. On the third of July, he lay in his bed dying. He knew this, and he tried hard to delay his final sleep so that he might see the dawn of Independence Day.

Waking from a feverish sleep, he asked the doctor, "Is it the Fourth?"

The doctor replied, "It will soon be."

All through the night he clung to life. When the light of dawn arrived he was satisfied, and at

Jefferson died on July 4, 1826, the 50th anniversary of the Declaration of Independence. The Jefferson Memorial in Washington, DC—dedicated on April 13, 1943, his 200th birthday—provides a lasting tribute to his leadership and vision.

fifty minutes past noon of July Fourth, 1826, he closed his eyes and his great warm heart grew cold.

Over the land the Stars and Stripes was flying, bells were ringing and cannons were booming in celebration of the signing of the Declaration of Independence.

And history records a strange coincidence. At that very moment in Quincy, Massachusetts, Jefferson's old friend, John Adams was also dying. He did not know that the Sage of Monticello had already gone. "Thomas Jefferson still survives," he said. These were his last words.

On the back of an old, torn letter Jefferson had written his own epitaph. It was found in a desk drawer. He asked that a modest stone obelisk be placed over his grave with "the following inscription, and not a word more."

HERE WAS BURIED

THOMAS JEFFERSON

AUTHOR OF THE DECLARATION OF INDEPENDENCE,

OF THE STATUTE OF VIRGINIA FOR RELIGIOUS FREEDOM,

AND FATHER OF THE UNIVERSITY OF VIRGINIA

And he added, "because of these, as testimonials that I have lived, I wish most to be remembered."

It was raining on the day they buried him in the family cemetry which he had laid out on the top of his "little mountain" close by his beautiful home. And his wish was carried out. The gray granite obelisk which marks his grave bears the modest inscription he desired "and not one word more."

For Further Reading

Bober, Natalie. *Thomas Jefferson: Man on a Mountain.* New York: Atheneum, 1988.

Morse, John T. *Thomas Jefferson.* New York: Chelsea House, 1981.

Patterson, Charles. *Thomas Jefferson.* New York: Watts, 1987.

Smith, Kathie. *Thomas Jefferson.* New York: Messner, 1989.

Index

Adams, John, 40, 56, 58, 60, 61, 64–66, 84, 86, 90, 91, 99, 107, 121–30, 144–45, 153
Albemarle County, 14–15, 31, 46, 78
Alien Act, 127–28, 133
America, 26, 47, 48–49, 66, 68, 86, 93, 117, 134
Assumption Bill, 108, 110

Barbary States, 139–40
Bastille, fall of, 95–96
Bill of Rights, 71, 97–98
Boston Port Bill, 44
Boston Tea Party, 43
Burr, Aaron, 128–29

Carr, Dabney, 16–17, 24, 40, 41, 42
Causes of Taking up Arms, 57
Clark, William, 137–38
Committees of Correspondence, 41–42, 43–44
Committees of Safety, 53
Common Sense, 59, 65
Confederation of Thirteen States, 88, 93; *see also* Thirteen Colonies, United States of America

Congress, Continental, 45–46, 49–50; First, 52; Second, 54–59, 61, 65–67, 85–89; *See also* Congress of the United States
Congress of the United States, 98, 107, 111, 127, 135, 137, 150; *see also* Congress, Continental
Constitution of the United States, 97–99, 106
Constitutional Convention, 97
Continental Army, 57, 69, 74, 78
Cornwallis, General, 73–74, 78

Declaration of Independence, 62–67, 95, 116, 152–53
Democrats, 116, 122, 127–28, 135

England, 7–9, 20, 26, 31–33, 38–39, 43–49, 51, 52–54, 57, 59–60, 65–66, 68, 73–75, 84–86, 87, 91, 114, 118, 125, 139–40
Europe, 85, 90, 93, 134, 139, 140, 148

Fauquier, Francis, 22, 32
Federalists, 107, 113–18, 121, 124–28, 133, 141

Index

France, 26, 73, 81, 85–86, 90–96, 98, 100, 106, 113, 114, 117, 125–26, 134–37, 140–41
Franklin, Benjamin, 56, 58, 61, 64–67, 68, 84, 86, 90–92, 104, 143
French and Indian War, 26
French Revolution, 95–96, 100, 113–14, 116–18
Funding Bill, 110

Gaspee, the, 38–39
Gazette of the United States, 113

Hamilton, Alexander, 107–18
Henry, Patrick, 19, 24, 26, 31, 32, 40, 44, 46, 49, 56, 72
House of Burgesses, 7, 15, 25–27, 31–33, 40–41, 44–46, 48, 55

Jay, John, 84, 106, 125
Jay's Treaty, 125
Jefferson, Elizabeth (sister), 13, 34
Jefferson, Jane (daughter), 58
Jefferson, Jane (sister), 13, 34
Jefferson, Jane Randolph (mother), 11–14, 34, 58
Jefferson, Lucy (sister), 34
Jefferson, Lucy Elizabeth (daughter), 84–85, 90, 98
Jefferson, Martha (daughter), 37, 74, 85–86, 90–91, 98–101, 103, 143, 151; later Mrs. Thomas Mann Randolph
Jefferson, Martha (sister), 34, 40, 43, 84; later Mrs. Dabney Carr
Jefferson, Martha Skelton (wife), 35–38, 42, 68, 72, 74, 84
Jefferson, Mary (daughter), 68, 72, 74, 85, 90, 98–99, 103; later Mrs. John Wayles Eppes
Jefferson, Mary (sister), 13, 34
Jefferson, Peter (father), 10–15

Jefferson, Randolph (brother), 16, 34
Jefferson Thomas,
 early life, 12–17
 attends college, 18–23
 studies law, 23–25
 practices law, 28
 plans and builds Monticello, 29–31, 35
 marriage, 37
 children, 37, 72, 84
 family deaths, 58
 as governor, 72–79
 in Congress, 86–89
 as Ambassador to France, 91–96
 as Secretary of State, 102–18
 as vice president, 124–25
 as president, 129–142
 builds University of Virginia, 146–48
 death of, 152–54

Lafayette, Marquis de, 76, 91, 148–49
Ledyard, John, 137
Lewis and Clark expedition, 138
Lewis, Meriwether, 137–38
Library of Congress, 150
Lord North's Conciliatory Proposition, 53, 55, 57
Louisiana, 26, 93, 134–37

Madison, James, 69, 71, 83, 97–98, 102, 114, 124, 128, 133, 151
Marshall, John, 130
Mason, George, 69, 71
Morris, Gouverneur, 87, 107
Monroe, James, 83, 99, 135–36, 142
Monticello, 28–31, 35, 37, 42–43, 58, 68–69, 80–84, 100–01, 103, 119–23, 132, 143–154

Napoleon, 134–35, 140
National Gazette, 113
New Orleans, *see* Louisiana
New York City, 99, 103–08
Notes on Virginia, 82

Page, John, 72
Paine, Thomas, 65, 113
Philadelphia, 46, 52, 55, 57, 58, 86, 97, 112
Potomac River, 108, 112, 129

Randolph, William, 11–13
religious freedom, 70–71
Republicans, 116
Revolutionary War, 56, 60, 73–76, 78
Richmond, Virginia, 56, 58, 75, 78, 94
rights of man, *see* Declaration of Independence
Rights of Man, The, 113
Romulus, the, 85

Sedition Act, 127–28, 133
Shadwell, 12, 14–17, 28, 34
slavery, 48, 66, 70, 89
Stamp Act of 1765, 26
Summary View of the Rights of British America, 46–51

taxation without representation, 26–27, 31–33
thirteen colonies, 25–27, 31–33, 38–42, 43–49, 52–53, 59–60, 64–65, 68, 71, 78; *see also* Confederation of Thirteen States; United States of America
Townshend Acts, 31–33, 43
Tuckahoe, 13–14, 74

United States of America, 68, 86, 97–100, 106–18, 125–28, 133–42, 152; *see also* thirteen colonies

Virginia and Kentucky Resolution, 128
Virginia Congress, 45–46, 49–50, 53; *see also* Virginia Convention
Virginia Convention, 54, 56, 58–59
Virginia Legislature, 68–71, 76–79
Virginia, University of, 145–48

Washington, D.C., 129, 151
Washington, George, 15, 31, 32, 49, 57, 65, 73, 75, 77, 78, 94, 97, 99, 100, 102, 103, 106, 114–18, 119
Wayles, John, 35, 42
Wythe, George, 22–23, 60, 67, 69